PERFECT
REDEMPTION

PERFECT REDEMPTION

The Purpose of
His Passion

DALE M. SIDES

The scripture used throughout this study is quoted from the King James Version unless otherwise noted. Bolded words within a verse indicates author's emphasis and any explanatory words inserted by the author are enclosed in brackets [ ].

PERFECT REDEMPTION
© 2004 by Dale M. Sides
ISBN 1-930433-21-2

Published by
Liberating Publications, Inc.
PO Box 974
Bedford, VA 24523-0974

Cover design and original artwork,
"Perfect Redemption," by Vicki Sides.
www.liberatingpublications.com

Printed in Colombia

Table of Contents

Table of Illustrations

Introduction

One night when I was teaching a class on *Perfect Redemption*, my good friend, Pastor Rick Stoker, said, "Let me make one more round and see if I can find anymore homeless people who want a good meal for their spirit and their body." About twenty minutes later he walked in the door with two men. I'll never forget the look on their faces. It was horrible. They were cold, dirty, and obviously very drunk. Rick had just retrieved them from underneath a railroad overpass. They had been drinking aftershave lotion.

I have seen the same look on people's faces in many different places around the world. I have seen it on high-caste, idol-worshiping Hindus in India. I have seen it on cannibals in Nigeria and prostitutes in Colombia. I have even seen the same look on the faces of committed Christians and church leaders. The look cries out for deliverance from inward pain. It is the same look, regardless of the country or language, and it does not matter what the person looks like on the outside: white, brown, black, clean, dirty, smiling, frowning, rich, or poor. The inside person—the spirit man or woman—cries, "Please, please, someone—please help me!"

I saw those two homeless men receive the Word of God regarding the blood of Jesus and they were freed that very night from the inward iniquity of lust and alcoholism. They applied just one of the ways that Jesus bled—it was the blood He shed when He was bruised for our iniquities. They are back with their families now. I saw one of the men just recently. He is married now to a former prostitute who has likewise been delivered and set free. They are testifying just like the madman from Gadara that Jesus Christ has set them free. Their inner torment and never-ending rage have been quieted. As Jesus said to the wind and storm, "Peace, be still," He quelled the storms raging on the inside of these men. He can do the same for you.

Please listen to me. As I learned the truths contained in this book and began teaching them, I started to see changes and deliverances in people as if I had discovered a miracle drug. In a way, I **did**! This is not a new drug but a fresh, new application of a timeless remedy—the blood of Jesus. I have stacks of testimonies and requests to come and teach these truths from all around the world. Personally, in five lifetimes I'll never be able to fill all these requests, so it is my hope that God will use the words I write to reach the farthest corners of the earth. May they help you personally and may they help you to help others, too. What I have seen and taught to thousands of people has worked for them and it will work for you, also.

In introduction, this new application of the blood of Jesus deals with two basic perspectives.

First, Jesus bled seven different ways and each way has a specific aspect of forgiveness and spiritual strengthening within it. This truth is so impacting that it drives demons out of people, restores physical healing to ailing bodies, and gives rest to wearied souls.

Second, the blood of Jesus has indeed been shed, but now we need to know *how* to apply it. As the blood of the Passover lamb was caught in a basin and then *applied* to the doorpost, we likewise need to apply the blood of Jesus—not to leave it in the basin.

I have noticed that in most Christians' spiritual medicine cabinets there is a bottle of unused faith. It is in a little brown bottle with a medicine dropper, stuck way back in the corner of the cabinet. They measure out faith in drops, trying to save some for the special remedy that would someday come. Now is the time to pull it out, dust it off, open it up, and use it. We all know that the blood of Jesus works; this is the remedy that really works. Now is the time to apply all the faith we have. Take off the top and mix your faith with the Word of God about the blood of Jesus (Hebrews 4:2).

May I be perfectly honest with you? If I did not have something of great value to share with you, I would not waste your time. God loves you and so do I. I beg you, please do not pass this off as just another topic among many. This works, and it will work as you work it. This is really going to help you, and those you love as you share it with them, too. Will you please pull that little bottle of unused faith out of the medicine cabinet and use it where you know it works—on the blood of Jesus?

It is unfortunate that most of what Christians know about the blood of Jesus is what we have learned from songs we have sung instead of the Word of God we have studied. No wonder so many Christians are still shackled to church pews. The Word of God testifies, "and ye shall know the truth, and the truth shall make you free," (John 8:32) so we must study the Word of God if we want the deliverance Jesus purchased for us. Romans 3:25 says that we are to have faith in the blood of Jesus, but instead we have had faith in our faith, or in a preacher's anointing, or in a new-fangled notion. What we simply need to do is study the Word of God about the blood of Jesus, see how the blood was shed, and then learn how to apply it.

To the end of understanding the seven ways that Jesus bled, *where* and *how* to apply the blood, I submit this work to you. It is presented for the uninstructed Christian who has little to no understanding of redemption, all the way to the most faithful believer who has struggled for years and years for deliverance. As *Perfect Redemption* would imply, it is complete—it starts new, remains fresh, and finishes strong.

PERFECT REDEMPTION

Jesus did not just bleed seven ways; He bled seven ways **for you**. You need to know these seven ways and how to apply the blood that He shed for you. As you learn this and apply these truths, you can receive Perfect Redemption. You can testify like the two homeless men, the madman from Gadara, and thousands of other Christians who have faithfully applied the blood of Jesus to the seven areas of their lives. You will be able to personally testify . . .

> *If the Son therefore shall make you free, ye shall be free indeed.*
>
> *John 8:36*

PART ONE

The Foundation of Redemption

T his portion of the book is written primarily for those who have little or no understanding of the Bible. The subject of redemption is the most basic truth of Christianity and its understanding will yield lifelong benefits. To build Christian understanding upon anything else could result in a faulty foundation. To have perfect redemption we must build upon a solid foundation. For those who are more spiritually nourished, a little review will not hurt you.

Reliable understanding is too often assumed, and the result of building upon a poor foundation is catastrophically predictable. Having a Bible does not equate with understanding it. Wouldn't it be nice if we could put it under our pillow and wake up renewed in the morning? As we examine these truths, keep in mind that the objective of education should not merely be knowledge—but action. The information given here will dovetail into action by applying the blood of Jesus to claim all that He has purchased for us. Then we can live as victorious, fulfilled, and perfectly redeemed Christians.

And for this cause he is the mediator of the new testament, that by means of death, for the redemption of the transgressions that were under the first testament, they which are called might receive the promise of eternal inheritance.

Hebrews 9:15

Chapter 1

What Is Redemption?

Redemption is the love story of God rescuing mankind. The story begins with God creating mankind, male and female, in the Garden of Eden to rule over His creation. Man turned his back on God, and gave his soul and the rulership that God gave him to God's archenemy—Satan. But God, Who is rich in mercy and love, saw the great pain in His creation and was moved with compassion. He offered His Son as a sacrifice to ransom mankind back to Himself.

Christianity is different from all other belief systems. It states that mankind is spiritually dead and separated from God (Ephesians 2:1–3), and that only a ransom being paid will reconcile them to God. This introduces the subject of redemption, which by dictionary definition means, "recovery by payment."[1] Jesus paid the price for the reconciliation—it was His blood.

God created Adam and Eve in perfect alignment and fellowship with Him. He gave them freedom of will and thereby allowed them to either maintain the fellowship through obedience, or lose it through disobedience. Through Satan's temptation and seduction of Eve, Adam transgressed and lost his perfect fellowship with God. Because God is just and legal, He had to "redeem" or purchase mankind back through another man. This man would have to be

PERFECT REDEMPTION

sinless and righteous in order to legally regain mankind and reconcile them to God. God's standard for ransom was not cheap: He required a blood sacrifice. He required blood—pure blood—as the payment for redemption.

God's plan for redemption was that Jesus Christ, God's only begotten Son, would be born into the world as our Savior. By Jesus' righteous life and sacrifice, He bought back the rights to mankind, both the living and the dead, away from the thief—Satan.

> *Who hath delivered us from the power of darkness,*
> *and hath translated us into the kingdom of his dear*
> *Son: In whom we have redemption through his*
> *blood, even the forgiveness of sins.*
> *Colossians 1:13–14*

Jesus' pure blood became the sacrificial payment for mankind's purchase. The blood of Jesus is how we are redeemed.

> *In whom **we have redemption through his blood**,*
> *the forgiveness of sins, according to the riches of his*
> *grace.*
> *Ephesians 1:7*

Notice that this verse says, "according to the riches of his grace." Grace means "favor, good will, or kindness."[2] This is exactly what the grace of God means—that God by His divine favor, not of mankind's merit or worthiness, sent a payment to ransom us and thereby reconciled His lost people back to Himself. It was God's mercy that prompted His gift of redemption. This perhaps helps to explain the most well-known verse in the Bible, John 3:16.

> *For God so loved the world, that he gave his only*
> *begotten Son, that whosoever believeth in him*
> *should not perish, but have everlasting life.*
> *John 3:16*

The free gift of God's grace means that when mankind embraces and accepts the goodness of God through Jesus Christ, they are forgiven of their sins and made righteous before God (Romans 3:21–25). This is the complete purchase of men and women back from Satan, removing all of Satan's rights and claims over them. This is God's doing because He wants us back. It is hard to believe that God would want us, but that's what love will do.

The study of redemption shows the depth of the sacrifice that Jesus Christ made by the shedding of His blood. This frees mankind from the grip of Satan and gives them back their full rights and privileges as God's children. This gift of grace from God has far greater ramifications than merely receiving a one-time present. Accepting grace can be compared to a child who receives a gift, plays with it awhile, then stuffs it in a toy box, never to play with it again. Truly receiving grace means to cherish and utilize it to its maximum potential.

> *All over the world this gospel is bearing fruit and growing, just as it has been doing among you since the day you heard it and understood God's grace in all its truth.*
>
> *Colossians 1:6 NIV*

Notice that we must understand the grace of God in all of its truth. This is similar to John 8:32, which says, "Ye shall know the truth, and the truth shall make you free." You must truly know it if you are going to receive its full benefit.

Studying *Perfect Redemption* will emphasize the deep impact of the blood of Jesus and the far-reaching effect it has in our lives. The title *Perfect Redemption* is derived from an old Christian hymn "Redeemed," which proclaims in the second verse, "O perfect redemption the purchase of blood, to every believer the promise of God." This is our promise!

The ransom has been paid by the grace of God. It is the blood of Jesus. Now we need to claim this gift by faith. Romans 10:17 states that faith comes by hearing and hearing by the Word of God. We need to hear the Word of God concerning the blood, not just to hear that it works, but to study it in order for it to work. Only then can we build our faith and apply the blood of Jesus in faith, according to the Word of God.

> Whom [Jesus Christ] God hath set forth to be a **propitiation through faith in his blood**, to declare his righteousness for the remission of sins that are past, through the forbearance of God.
>
> *Romans 3:25*

The life of Jesus Christ was the gift of God's grace. As we receive this gift and understand the grace of God in all its truth, we can stand in faith to claim what Jesus' blood accomplished. It is vitally important to study the attributes of the blood sacrifice that Jesus made and everything it redeemed—including health, prosperity, and our fellowship with God. We want to reclaim all that Jesus purchased for us. This is how we can receive the full effect of redemption.

Mankind struggled under the curse and dominion of Satan for approximately 4,000 years before the coming of Jesus Christ and the payment of His blood. Even before Jesus' coming, God wanted freedom for His people and to have fellowship with them despite the betrayal and separation. He instituted a covenant whereby He could help His fallen creatures, but it was only until the time when full restitution could be made. This was the Old Testament or Old Covenant.

> And for this cause [of redemption] he [Jesus] is the mediator of the new testament, that by means of death, for the redemption of the transgressions that were under the first testament, they which are called might receive the promise of eternal inheritance.
>
> *Hebrews 9:15*

Even in the Old Testament God required a blood sacrifice to be offered for mankind to enter into fellowship with Him. The blood He required was not sufficient for the promise of eternal inheritance; it was only good enough to moderately repair the fellowship between the Father God and His children. He was looking forward to the day when the separation would be permanently reconciled. When the payment of the blood of Jesus was offered, God **made** redemption unto us. He gave to us a gift to reconcile us to Himself.

> *But of him are ye in Christ Jesus, who of God is made unto us wisdom, and righteousness, and sanctification, and redemption.*
>
> *1 Corinthians 1:30*

This is the free gift of redemption; it has already been made unto us by the shedding of the blood of Jesus. **Our dilemma now is not to get redemption, but to claim it**. This is our quest in our study: to discover the depth of redemption and realize that our full recovery has been paid for—that Jesus bled seven different ways to pay for us to be fully reconciled to God. Redemption, by the grace of God, has already been made unto us; now we need to claim it.

Our enemy has demonstrated time and time again that he does not respect the covenants of God. He will not release his control over us unless we claim our full authority and rights as redeemed Christians. Redemption is ours. We do not wrestle for it, but we wrestle to claim it. As we learn of our God-given rights and the freedom that the blood of Jesus purchased for us, we will grow in our faith and assertion of the New Covenant rights and privileges we have. Christ Jesus was made redemption for us. Now we must learn and grow in our faith to appropriate what has already been purchased for us.

Basic Definitions Relating to Redemption

Too often the subject of redemption is not built upon a sound foundation because biblical terminology is not well understood. Likewise, related terms such as *reconciliation* and *atonement* are often confused because they are not well defined. The following story and metaphorical explanation has helped thousands of people to understand and remember the definition of redemption.

Once upon a time a father and his son built a small, toy boat. The longer they worked on it, the more proud they became of their workmanship. They painted it red, white, and blue, put a sail and a rudder on it, stenciled their names on the side of it, and christened it for its maiden voyage. When they slid it into the water at a nearby creek, they beamed with pride as the boat skidded sleekly across the water.

While they were admiring their creation, to their horror, a small whirlwind whisked past them, engulfed the tiny ship, and spun it round and round. Much to their pleasure, the boat did not sink. Much to their dismay, however, the boat headed downstream and disappeared from sight.

They were heartbroken. Their masterpiece was gone.

Sometime later, the son was visiting a town that was downstream from their home doing business for his father. Walking past a store, he spied his boat in the window. He could hardly believe his good fortune. With no reservation he rushed into the store and picked up the boat. As he examined it, he could see the consequences of what had happened during their separation. There were nicks and gouges on the boat and places where the paint had worn, but at least the father and son's names were still boldly stenciled on the side.

As he was admiring the boat, thankful for finding his lost masterpiece, someone interrupted his musings. The stern voice of the store proprietor spoke to him and asked, "May I help you?" As the young man raised his eyes to meet the storekeeper's, the exchange was not warm. Instead there was a foreboding look of disapproval on the storekeeper's face.

What is Redemption?

The young man's voice quivered as he spoke, "This, ah, this is my boat." His voice trailed off at the end. He continued, "My father and I built this together and when we were sailing it, a whirlwind separated it from us and it floated downstream. I'm so glad I found it," he said. "I can hardly believe I found it. My father will be so glad. Look," he said, as he pointed to the names clearly stenciled on the side, "these are our names. It really is ours."

The storekeeper hardly blinked at the excitement of the young man. He did not share in the thrill of the reunion. He coldly asserted, "You might claim this is your boat, but I found it in the stream. It was deserted and capsized. I fished it out, fixed it up, and now it is mine. You may say it's yours, but the only way you're walking out of here with it is to pay me for it." The young man could see the scratches and gouges on the boat and knew that no fixing up had been done, but he could not deny that someone had found it and it was in his store for sale.

Realizing he would be paying for something that was already his, the son asked, "How much do you want for it?" The storekeeper replied, "Twenty dollars is the price. Take it or leave it." The young man fondled a neatly folded twenty-dollar bill in his pocket. His father had given it to him to buy some supplies. It belonged to his father, but the son knew what he had to do. It was all he had.

He pulled the money out of his pocket, pushed it into the storekeeper's sweaty hand, looked him straight in the eye and boldly declared, "I'll take it. You know the boat rightfully belongs to me. Now it is legally mine again." Without another word, he adamantly whirled around, walked out of the store, and headed home to bring the boat back to his father.

This story illustrates separation, redemption, reconciliation, and atonement. Our Heavenly Father, Yahweh, is represented as the father, Jesus as the son, the devil as the storekeeper, the deception of Adam as the whirlwind, and you are the boat. The price the son paid represents the blood of Jesus. In reality, Jesus gave His life for you to be reconciled to God, and He did it by bleeding to death. He paid all that He had. Though you were once separated, now you are reconciled to God.

Redemption indicates a price paid for something. In this instance, it meant buying something back that was already owned. The duration of time the boat was gone represents the separation between mankind and God. When the boat was purchased, it was reconciled back to its rightful owner. Once it was reconciled, it was atoned with its owner. When Jesus paid for you with His blood, He bought you back from the devil. You no longer belong to Satan.

> *Who [God the Father] hath delivered us from the power of darkness, and hath translated us into the kingdom of his dear Son: In whom we have redemption through his blood, even the forgiveness of sins.*
> *Colossians 1:13–14*

The blood that Jesus shed came out of Him in seven different places. There is a truth revealed within the numerics of Scripture that is worthy to note.[3] The number seven indicates both spiritual perfection and covenant promise. God's perfect order and covenant with mankind has been sealed in the blood of Jesus. The blood of Jesus banishes three kinds of wrongs, and the number three means completeness. A complete work was done on Calvary. The blood of Jesus was shed in payment for you to be reconciled to God and to forgive you in seven different ways. Through complete redemption, a perfect covenant relationship is established with God again. Once you have been reconciled, you have received the atonement.

The actual breakdown of the word "atonement" demonstrates its definition. At-one-ment is the true meaning of this word. Jesus came to make us **at one** with God.

> *That they all may be one; as thou, Father, art in me,
> and I in thee, **that they also may be one in us**: that
> the world may believe that thou hast sent me. And
> the glory which thou gavest me I have given them;
> **that they may be one, even as we are one**: I in them,
> and thou in me, **that they may be made perfect in
> one**; and that the world may know that thou hast
> sent me, and hast loved them, as thou hast loved me.*
> *John 17:21–23*

When Jesus shed His blood for you, He paid for you to be at one
with God. In regards to the analogy of the boat, Jesus did not leave
any part of you in the store with the devil. You may have some scuff
marks and peeled painted, but you now belong to the Master who
has all the tools and love required to make repairs.

This is the whole story of redemption. Jesus gave everything He
had to reconcile you with the Father. You may have been separated
in the past, but now, by the grace of God—**you are redeemed.**

They must know that they have been
redeemed and what that redemption
signified, but they must above all
know that "it was not by corruptible
things such as silver and gold,"
things in which there was no power
of life, "but by the precious blood of
Christ." To have a correct perception
of what the preciousness of that
blood was (as the power of a perfect
redemption), would be to them the
power of a new and holy life."

Andrew Murray (The Power of the Blood of Jesus)

Chapter 2

Why Is the Blood of Jesus
Needed for Redemption?

B lood is the ultimate sacrifice. Leviticus 17:11 clearly states that the life of the flesh is in the blood, so when a blood sacrifice is required, life is offered and the ultimate commitment is made.

> *For the life of the flesh is in the blood: and I have given it to you upon the altar to make an atonement for your souls: for it is the blood that maketh an atonement for the soul.*
>
> *Leviticus 17:11*

Most cultures have ceremonial events involving blood: drinking it, shedding one's own blood, or the shedding of a substitute's blood. Each of these acts depicts sacrifice and unreserved commitment.

How commitment and sacrifice are related is told in a story regarding a chicken and a pig. One day the chicken and the pig were having a discussion about how people do not appreciate a breakfast of ham and eggs. The chicken said, "People do not appreciate the hard work it takes to lay an egg. It hurts and takes great effort to lay an egg." The pig said, "That's the difference between ham and eggs. It takes commitment to lay an egg, but it takes sacrifice to supply the ham."

God required both commitment and sacrifice for mankind to be redeemed. Many people before the time of Christ were committed to the death, but they could not offer the sacrifice. Why was it only the blood of Jesus that could redeem mankind and reconcile them to God?

God's desire to have fellowship with mankind was so great that He instituted a blood sacrifice even before the Redeemer came. It involved the shedding of the blood of animals, particularly of bulls, goats, lambs, and doves. Subjective reasoning tells us that each animal's attributes illustrates an aspect of forgiveness that God extended when each one's blood was shed. These sacrifices were necessary in order for God to re-institute what was lost by Adam's transgression. The blood of bulls was shed to indicate God's forgiveness for lack of strength; goat's blood represented God's forgiveness of stubbornness or rebellion; lamb's blood demonstrated God's forgiveness for independence, and dove's blood was shed for forgiveness and purification.

Hebrews 10:4 clearly verifies that these animal sacrifices were not sufficient for God's plan of redemption. They were only temporary until the ultimate sacrifice could be made.

> *For it is not possible that the blood of bulls and of goats should take away sins.*[4]
>
> *Hebrews 10:4*

God needed the blood of a man, not of an animal, for perfect redemption. When mankind lost relationship with God through the transgression of Adam, it became imperative that another man would have to offer the ultimate sacrifice to reconcile mankind with God. The sacrifice was the life of that individual and the representation of that life was his blood. What God required, however, was not just any blood: it had to be the blood of a sinless and righteous man and it had to be pure. **It had to be the blood of Jesus.** The blood of Jesus was the only blood that would suffice. A brief lesson in physiology and the mechanics of hematology (the study of blood) will help us to understand why it had to be Jesus' blood, and

Why is the Blood of Jesus Needed for Redemption?

only His blood, that could redeem us.

Hematology tells us that the blood of a child is determined and contributed from the male chromosome, not the female. In actuality, the mother's blood never intermingles with the blood of the fetus. The baby is fed through capillary exchange when the placenta transfers nutrients into the baby's blood. When the Holy Spirit overshadowed Mary (Luke 1:35) and impregnated her, the contribution of the male side of the chromosomes came from God through the Holy Spirit. In other words, the blood of Jesus came from God and was not contaminated by the sin-tainted blood of mankind. Jesus' blood was perfectly pure and never intermingled with Mary's or the blood of any man.

Hebrews 2:14 declares that children are partakers of flesh and blood, but Jesus only took part.[5] The part that He took was of the flesh. He got the flesh from Mary, but His blood came from God. That is why His blood was pure. Only the blood of Jesus was a pure, uncontaminated sacrifice that could redeem mankind. Only His blood can reconcile mankind to God and restore the covenant that Adam once enjoyed.

Jesus' pure blood forgives the weakness that the bull's blood represented; it avails forgiveness for rebellion and stubbornness that the goat portrayed; it forgives mankind's independence that the lamb's blood typified, and establishes the purification of mankind that the blood of the dove demonstrated.

Jesus' Blood Was His Offering to Qualify Himself as High Priest

The blood of Jesus was shed not only for us to be forgiven, but also, the shedding of His blood qualified Him as the High Priest of all ages. If most people were asked what is Jesus' job description today, they would say, "He is Savior." Although this is technically true, He "was" Savior because He already paid the price for our salvation. More accurately, Jesus Christ's function now is High Priest. He came as Savior and then shed His blood to qualify Himself for the function and office of High Priest.

In Leviticus 16 the ordinance is enacted for the Day of Atonement. On that day the blood of bulls and goats was shed for particular reasons. Understanding the significance of each of these sacrifices will emphasize why only the blood of Jesus could redeem mankind.

The blood of the bull was shed in order to purify the High Priest and allow him to enter into the Holy of Holies to offer sacrifice for the people. The blood of the goat was then applied to forgive the sins, transgressions, and iniquities of the people of Israel. (See also Hebrews 9:7.)

> *And Aaron shall bring the bullock of the sin offering, which is for himself, and shall make an atonement for himself, and for his house,* **and shall kill the bullock of the sin offering which is for himself.**
>
> *Leviticus 16:11*

> *Then shall he kill* **the goat of the sin offering, that is for the people,** *and bring his blood within the vail, and do with that blood as he did with the blood of the bullock, and sprinkle it upon the mercy seat, and before the mercy seat.*
>
> *Leviticus 16:15*

Before Jesus could represent us before God as High Priest to make intercession for the forgiveness of our sins, He had to gain access to the Father. The shedding of His blood made this available. This correlates to the blood of the bull. It purified and qualified Him as the High Priest.

> *Then He said, "Behold, I have come to do Your will, O God." He takes away the first [offering of bulls and goats] that He may establish the second [offering of His own blood]. By that will [God's will] we*

Why Is the Blood of Jesus Needed for Redemption?

have been sanctified through the offering of the body
of Jesus Christ once for all.

Hebrews 10:9–10 NKJ

In the Old Testament, once the High Priest was purified by the blood of the bull, he was then qualified to make an offering for the sins of the people. This is exactly what Jesus did because of the blood He shed. Jesus can and does now function as High Priest and appears in the presence of God for us.

For Christ is not entered into the holy places made
with hands, which are the figures of the true; but
into heaven itself, now to appear in the presence of
God for us:

Hebrews 9:24

We have a Savior that can be touched with the feelings of our infirmities. He goes before God to plead mercy for us (Hebrews 4:15–16). As we press into the reality of the blood of Jesus, we see there are two vital aspects of His blood: (1) it was shed, (2) it needs to be applied. Foreshadowing Part Four of this book, we will see that the blood of Jesus is applied only through confession. When we confess Jesus on the earth, He—as our High Priest—confesses us before the Father in heaven.

Therefore, holy brethren, partakers of the heavenly
calling, consider the Apostle and High Priest of our
confession, Christ Jesus.

Hebrews 3:1 NKJ

When we apply the blood of Jesus, we are accessing His ministry as High Priest. Jesus is kneeling and making intercession for us *now* before the throne of God. When our offenses are abolished and our account is cleared, He dispatches ministering spirits to bring us our spiritual blessings that are in the heavenly places (Ephesians 1:3).[6]

All of these things are available because of the blood shed by Jesus. He shed it to be qualified as High Priest in order to enter into the presence of God for us. He also shed His blood so that He could, as High Priest, make intercession for us. It was the shedding of His own blood that enabled Him to fulfill this role in intercession and mediation between God and man (1 Timothy 2:5).

Our Covenant with God

There is a word used in the Bible that should attract the attention of every Christian. It is the word "covenant." By definition, this word means a binding agreement or a compact. With biblical significance, it means the contracted agreement God has made with mankind. Understanding the word "covenant" reveals the contract arrangement God makes with people and lays the foundation upon which our faith can be built.

Covenant is used over 270 times in the Old Testament. Oddly enough (via the King James translation) it is only used eighteen times in the New Testament. The reason it is used so few times in the New Testament is because God did not change the benefits or consequences of abiding by it or breaking it when the new one came. The main thing that changed was the standard by which one enters into it. The Old Covenant required the blood of bulls and goats to be applied by a high priest as he confessed the sins, iniquities, and transgressions of the children of Israel. The New Covenant is engaged by the blood of Jesus as applied by our High Priest.

The keeping of both the Old and New Covenants yielded/yields the rich blessings of God called "the blessing of Abraham." These blessings included/include fellowship with God, health, longevity, prosperity, and of course eternal life. Simply stated, it is the favor of God. Leviticus 26:42, a very important verse of Scripture that will be covered in depth later, illustrates the blessing of the covenant of Abraham when a believer in the Old Testament adhered

Why Is the Blood of Jesus Needed for Redemption?

to his part of the agreement. Galatians 3:14 documents that this same covenant promise applies to the New Testament saints also.

> *Then will I remember my covenant with Jacob, and also my covenant with Isaac, and also my **covenant with Abraham** will I remember; and I will remember the land.*
>
> *Leviticus 26:42*

> *That the **blessing of Abraham** might come on the Gentiles through Jesus Christ; that we might receive the promise of the Spirit through faith.*
>
> *Galatians 3:14*

These blessings are a gift of God's grace and can never be earned. They are available to everyone who calls upon the name of the Lord and fulfills the requirements He has asked. This is the contract arrangement that God has stipulated.

Our New Testament bargain and arrangement with God is now based upon the blood of Jesus. Luke 22:20, along with other verses, asserts this truth.

> *Likewise He also took the cup after supper, saying, "This cup is the new covenant in My blood, which is shed for you.*
>
> *Luke 22:20 NKJ*

The foundation of our covenant arrangement with God is the shed blood of Jesus. A problem arises when we do not know the stipulations God has required of us to uphold the agreement. Particularly, how do we *apply* the blood of Jesus? This is what we need to fully understand! Only then can we make a demand upon our faith to expect (with full assurance of faith) the blessings of God, and the covenant blessing of Abraham to come upon us and overtake us.

This is the God-ordained covenant with the world today. It is accomplished only through the blood of Jesus Christ. It is as valid and powerful today as it was when the blood was shed at Calvary.

Our responsibility within the covenant is to know what is required of us, i.e., how to apply it, and then we can expect to see its many blessings come forth.

The Blood of Jesus Was Shed for the Forgiveness of Sins

Forgiveness is one of the greatest elements the blood of Jesus offers us. John 14:6 tells us that Jesus is the way, the truth, and the life and that no man can come to the Father but by Him. Only Jesus can bring us into the presence of God because it is His blood that removes our sins, iniquities, and transgressions. Appearing in the presence of God is only possible because of the forgiveness His blood extends to us.

> *But your iniquities have separated between you and your God, and your sins have hid his face from you, that he will not hear.*
>
> *Isaiah 59:2*

Only the blood of Jesus removes the offenses that separate us from God, gives us forgiveness, and allows us to come into His presence.

> *In whom we have redemption through his blood, the forgiveness of sins, according to the riches of his grace;*
>
> *Ephesians 1:7*

The blood of Jesus paralyzes all evil spirits, demons, principalities, and powers because it is His blood that removes sin, iniquity, and transgression from us. These are the offenses that give evil spirits authority over us. His blood terrifies these spiritual forces because it removes the demonic "handhold" or "foothold" from people.

I have witnessed the power of the blood of Jesus many, many times. I've witnessed how it removes offenses and the presence of demons in a person's life. Once, as I was conducting a deliverance session,

Why Is the Blood of Jesus Needed for Redemption?

there was a young man in the class who was being held by demons. They would not come out of him. I walked over to the man and addressed the demons and said, "The blood of Jesus has covered this man and you have no right over him." The demon spoke back to me using the man's voice but with a coarse, guttural utterance and said, "He belongs to me because of the blood put on the altar and I do not have to come out."

I knew, by the Holy Spirit, there had been an occasion when this man was offered to Satan through a blood sacrifice in a satanic worship ritual. (I have mentioned before that blood sacrifices are used in many worship contexts.) I commanded the demon to shut up, and asked the man if he had been involved in satanic worship. He told me that his father had dedicated him to Satan when he was a child by cutting him and spilling his blood on the satanic altar. I told the man to repent of the sin.

He said, "The blood of Jesus has cleansed me from this sin. It is stronger than my blood and the Spirit of the Lord is more powerful than any demon." Then the man said, "By the blood of Jesus, I command you foul spirit to come out of me." The demon came out of him with a loud roar, convulsing him and throwing him about. After the demon left, the man was lying face down on the floor— delivered and praising the Lord who had freed him by the blood of Jesus. *That* is how to apply the blood of Jesus and remove the access that demons have.

When sins, iniquities, and transgressions (see Part Three) are covered by the blood of Jesus, they are forgiven. There is no longer a place for demons to invade a person, nor any place for principalities or powers to torment people. Colossians 2:14 and 15 declare that Jesus spoiled principalities and powers and triumphed over them by the power of the cross. This is because the blood of Jesus forgives offenses and when they are forgiven, evil spirits have no legal access to a person through them.

Let me repeat this again. **Sins, iniquities, and transgressions give evil spirits authority over you.** It has taken me over twenty-five years to figure this statement out and to make it in such a simple form. I have seen many, many people be delivered from the torment of evil spirits since I came to this understanding. This information directly relates to Ephesians 4:27, where it says to give no place to the devil.

In conclusion, the blood of Jesus is the only blood that can redeem mankind. It alone is pure; it alone qualified Him as High Priest; it alone was shed for our New Covenant relationship, and it alone forgives our sins, iniquities, and transgressions.

Chapter 3

The Blood Shed AND
The Blood Applied

If the statement were made, "The blood of Jesus works." there would probably be unanimous agreement in most Christian churches throughout the world. But considering that as many as 75 percent of the people answering the question are classified lukewarm by their pastors, it should make us take another look. If the blood of Jesus works and delivers people, then why are so many Christians failing to experience this victory? Why are they still living in bondage?

The answer is simple. The blood of Jesus does work, but there is great difference between the blood being shed and the blood being applied. The great gap in our understanding is that the blood of Jesus, as powerful and impacting as it is, is ineffective for deliverance unless we apply it. The blood was shed—now it needs to be applied.

I have a very good friend and fellow minister from Radcliff, Kentucky whose name is Larry Coker. Larry has a powerful deliverance ministry and has assisted me in many overseas trips to India. We have ministered healing to more people and cast out more demons together than "there are cows in Texas." In years past, we have discussed why Christians are in such a dire state when we know that the blood of Jesus works. We concluded that the problem is not in the power of the blood, but in knowing how to apply it.

In chapter 2, from the Old Covenant perspective, we discussed the blood of bulls and goats being used to cover the sins, iniquities, and transgressions of the children of Israel on the Day of Atonement. The bull and the goat were killed at the door of the tabernacle and their blood was collected. This is the point where the blood was shed, but certainly the sacrifice did not end there. It began there. The high priest next had to sprinkle the blood of the sacrifice before the mercy seat seven times (Leviticus 16:14–15). It is the sprinkling of the blood that specifically demonstrates how the blood was applied.

There is another feast day of the Lord that illustrates the exact same truth of the blood needing to be applied—the Passover. In the Passover memorial, the lamb was slain by cutting its throat and its blood was collected in a basin. The blood then was applied to the two door posts and the overhead lintel.

> *And ye shall take a bunch of hyssop, and dip it in the blood that is in the bason, and **strike the lintel and the two side posts** with the blood that is in the bason; and none of you shall go out at the door of his house until the morning.*
>
> *Exodus 12:22*

The blood was collected in a basin and then *struck* or applied to the door. The three places where it was applied parallels the three kinds of wrongs that the blood forgives. These wrongs are sins, iniquities, and transgressions.

On the eventful night of the first Passover, I would imagine the children of Israel were very careful to apply the blood to the three parts of the door. No one stood around and said, "Well, we have the blood. That should do." No! They *applied* the blood to the door to receive protection from the Passover angel. Fear was then as fear is now. They applied the blood.

The Blood Shed AND The Blood Applied

The applications of the blood on the Day of Atonement and the Passover show us specifically where the blood is to be applied. On the Day of Atonement, the blood was applied directly before the mercy seat seven times for reconciliation and atonement. On Passover, the blood was applied to three places directly on the door, for fellowship and healing. There is a magnificent truth revealed when we understand the application of the blood on the Day of Atonement and Passover. The blood applied on the Day of Atonement was for reconciliation. The blood applied on the Passover was for forgiveness. However, regardless of what it was applied for, it had to be applied.

The New Covenant perspective is just as valid for applying the blood.

> *Likewise also the cup after supper, saying, This cup*
> *is the new testament in my blood, which is shed for*
> *you.*
>
> *Luke 22:20*

How effective do you think even the blood of Jesus would have been if the apostles merely looked at the cup and then walked away without drinking from it? Peter, James, John, and the eight other apostles applied what was given to them and they received the blessings of God. However, Judas Iscariot did not drink from the cup and did not receive the benefits. **The blood of Jesus has to be applied if it is going to be effective.**

As I have ministered these truths in many places, I have come to realize that Christians are not usually rebellious in refusing to apply the blood. The problem is that they have not been taught how or where to apply the blood. When Christians are not reconciled to God in a particular aspect of their lives, they need to understand the seven ways Jesus bled. Then they need to apply His blood to their sin, iniquity and transgression through confessing to their High Priest.

PERFECT REDEMPTION

The great Evangelist Billy Graham once said that Christians were stuck between Calvary and the Upper Room. My addition to this statement is that we are stuck between the basin and the doorpost, or between the blood of the goat and the sprinkling before the mercy seat, or between the cup and the drinking. We have the blood—we just need to *apply* it.

We are now ready to gain an understanding of "The Blood Shed," where we will explore the ways Jesus bled. Be informed however, that even this information alone will not bring you perfect redemption without knowing how or where to apply the blood.

This section, Part One, "The Foundation of Redemption," has been offered to give definitions and explanations for the novice more so than for the mature Christian. As we move into the following sections of this book, no more distinctions will be made because we have established the foundation and we are now all on the same floor—we all have sinned and come short of the glory of God (Romans 3:23). Whether you are recently born again or have been counted in the household of faith for years and years, only the blood of Jesus is what gives you access into the presence of God and forgiveness for your wrong doings. The blood shed *and* the blood applied must *both* be studied, understood, and then properly utilized.

PART TWO

The Blood Shed

Leviticus 16:14 and 15 prophetically profile the sacrifice of Jesus Christ in its illustration of the high priest sprinkling the blood of bulls and goats before the mercy seat seven times. Each time the high priest sprinkled the blood, although the action of sprinkling was the same, seven different aspects of the blood being shed were indicated. This comparison emphasizes that although the blood of Jesus was the same pure blood, He bled seven different ways to accomplish our perfect redemption.

To increase our faith in the blood (Romans 3:25), we need to study each particular way Jesus bled and the significance it yields concerning forgiveness, reconciliation and righteousness. As we gain knowledge regarding each of the different ways He bled, we will also see that He did not bleed for us just to be forgiven, but Jesus bled in order for us to be reinstated in the authority of the covenant of Adam, as well as the blessing of the covenant of Abraham. Jesus came not only for us to be forgiven, but also for us to be able to reign in life (Romans 5:17).

Because of the significance of the way Jesus died, the next chapter, "The Anatomy of the Crucifixion," will demonstrate the different ways that Jesus bled. God prophetically planned each way Jesus was to shed His blood. In addition, we will gain a deeper appreciation for the agony and pain He experienced in order to redeem us and reconcile us to the Father.

In these next two chapters we are going to deal with the horrible death of Jesus of Nazareth. As we cover the graphic details of His death and suffering by crucifixion, may the Holy Spirit revisit the event to you so that you can come to understand and appreciate what Jesus did for you. This is not meant to be grotesque, but it does have a salient point.

One might say, "Why do I need to conceptualize the details of the crucifixion? Can't I just accept the forgiveness?" The answer is that when crucifixions were carried out, it was for a purpose—to shock the spectators with gruesome horror and to set an example of what happens to people who commit such punishable offenses. The execution of Jesus of Nazareth was intended by God and man to be portrayed in the full extent of its ugliness in order to impact the onlookers. We are supposed to look and relate to His pain, because He was the substitute for us. He took our place on the cross.

Forgiveness is a spiritual reality. We receive it from God whenever we apply the blood of Jesus. Sometimes, however, we hold on to the memories of what we did long after the spiritual forgiveness has been granted. When we have the graphic details of His crucifixion imprinted in our minds, rather than recalling the memories of our sins, we can recall the image of His suffering and the price He paid for the sin. Rather than recalling the horrible things we did with our hands, we can recall the nail piercing the median nerve in the wrist of the Messiah, blood spurting out of the hole and his hand clenching into a claw. Yes, we can readily confess that Jesus was our substitute and took our place on the cross, but the reality draws closer when the images are fixed in our minds.

Although we all want to know the power of His resurrection, God tells us in Philippians 3:10 that there is more He wants us to know.

> *That I may know him, and the power of his resur-*
> *rection, and the fellowship of his sufferings, being*
> *made conformable unto his death;*
>
> *Philippians 3:10*

The aspect of "being made conformable unto His death" is available by accepting His death; but to fully receive the benefits of His sufferings, we need the details of His death at the crucifixion firmly implanted in our minds. We have not done Christianity any favor by cleaning up the cross at Calvary. We have robbed ourselves of the right to identify with Jesus' sufferings.

When plaguing thoughts of past transgressions or sins come to your consciousness, whether by association or demonic reminder, replace them with the graphic details of the crucifixion. Accept Jesus as your substitute for sin—not just death. He bore our sorrow and our grief. He was stricken and smitten of God—afflicted so the chastisement of our peace could be laid upon Him.

As the facts and the truths of the crucifixion are covered in these next two chapters, may you more fully realize and accept the fellowship of His sufferings and be made conformable to His death.

My strength is dried up like a potsherd; and my tongue cleaveth to my jaws; and thou hast brought me into the dust of death. For dogs have compassed me: the assembly of the wicked have inclosed me: they pierced my hands and my feet.

Psalm 22:15–16

Chapter 4

The Anatomy of
the Crucifixion

Crucifixion is the most horrible and painful method of execution ever devised. It is one thing to execute a criminal for committing a capital crime, but it's another thing altogether for mankind to violate the sixth commandment of God, "You shall not murder," by taking pleasure in it and sadistically dragging it out for the enjoyment of the spectators and the executioners.

Crucifixions, particularly the way they were carried out during Jesus' time, had been developed over many centuries. The Persians were the first to begin, the Greeks then practiced it, and finally the Romans perfected it. Regardless of the society involved, only the most hardened criminals were executed in this manner, and it was calculated to make a statement to the general public. It was meant to be a spectacle of horror and lasting impact.

The Persians' preferred way of execution was to drop the victim on a sharpened stake, piercing the entrails and leaving the person to die in a relatively short time. As the Greek civilization ascended, this form of execution was further developed by piercing the abdomen and pulling the small intestine out. However, it was the Romans who developed crucifixion into a scientific method of pain and prolonged death.

Many of the details known about crucifixion can be attributed to corpses that have been discovered during archeological digs in the area of Palestine. Putting these details together with information from the Scriptures makes it possible to reach some conclusions.

The actual cause of death in a crucifixion was a combination of the loss of blood and asphyxiation.[7] Crucifixion's specific aim was to extend the time of suffering and death. By not severing any major veins or arteries, but by inflicting only flesh and muscular wounds, the executioner intended that the victim would slowly bleed to death. The combined aspect of asphyxiation was caused by tying a rope about the waist, which allowed for the victim's weight to be supported by the rope, rather than hanging from the nail wounds in the hands and feet. As the victim would approach unconsciousness, due to shallow and painful breathing, he would have to pull himself up and stand on the nails in order to release the pressure of the rope on his diaphragm. He could then expel the buildup of carbon dioxide, and inhale oxygen. In addition to growing weaker and weaker from the loss of blood, the victim would grow confused and disoriented because of the excess carbon dioxide in the blood stream. This is illustrated in the following chart.

The Anatomy of the Crucifixion

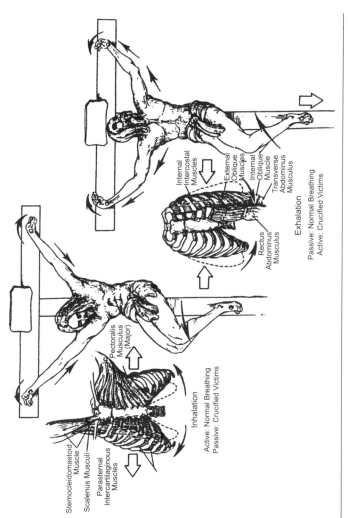

Respirations during crucifixion. Left, Inhalation. With elbows extended and shoulders abducted, respiratory muscles of inhalation are passively stretched and thorax is expanded. Right, Exhalation. With elbows flexed and shoulders adducted and with weight of body on nailed feet, exhalaion is accomplished as active, rather than passive, process. Breaking legs below knees would place burden of exhalation on shoulder and arm muscles alone and soon would result in exhaustion asphyxia.

Sternocleidomastoid Muscle
Scalenus Musculi
Parasternal Intercartilaginous Muscles

Inhalation
Active: Normal Breathing
Passive: Crucified Victims

Pectoralis Musculus (Major)

Internal Intercostal Muscles
External Oblique Muscles
Internal Oblique Muscle
Transverse Abdominus Musculus
Rectus Abdominus Musculus

Exhalation
Passive: Normal Breathing
Active: Crucified Victims

(This chart courtesy of the *Journal of the American Medical Association*, March 21, 1986, Vol. 255, No. 11, "On the Physical Death of Jesus Christ," pp. 1455–1463.)

More often than not, a crucifixion would last for days and days. Pilate marveled that Jesus died so soon (Mark 15:44). The reason Jesus expired so quickly was due to His weakened state from the beatings He received before He was nailed to the cross. We have an idea of the possible duration of the crucifixion due to a quotation from the Book of Psalms, where it speaks of the dogs having compassed Jesus. It was common at that time for wild dogs to tear at the flesh and eat the victims (while still alive) when the crowds were not present, especially at night.

> *My strength is dried up like a potsherd; and my tongue cleaveth to my jaws; and thou hast brought me into the dust of death.* ***For dogs have compassed me****: the assembly of the wicked have inclosed me: they pierced my hands and my feet.*
>
> *Psalm 22:15–16*

Even though we often accept that the crucifixion began with nailing the hands and feet to the cross, this is not the case, and the seven ways that Jesus bled will bear this out. The actual "art form" of crucifixion began with beating and scourging. The aim was to weaken the victim with shock due to loss of blood by the beating on the back. (There was an additional function for the lacerated back—to scrub against the vertical cross member while on the cross.)

The beatings were done with whips, or as some people call them, "a cat of nine tails." It was a scourge with pieces of bone or metal woven into the tip of each strand. The first slash cut; the second one ripped; the third one tore and from then on, each lash literally pulled tissue out of the back. The executioner was trained to stop just short of the victim passing out due to pain and loss of blood.

I have heard people speculate that Jesus was beaten with thirty-nine lashes. Be reminded that this was a Jewish law. Jesus was crucified by Romans who knew or kept no such custom. They beat Him to within an "nth" degree of His life. The severity of the beatings directly attributed to the relatively short length of time Jesus actually hung on the cross. When the devil got his hands on Jesus, he beat him and beat him and beat him and beat him. When they put the crown of thorns on His head and the purple robe on His back, the robe was only purple for a short time. It would have quickly become red from the blood that oozed out of His back.

Most of the blood loss in crucifixions came from the wounds on the back. In addition, when the executioners nailed the victim to the cross, they threw him on the ground, which rubbed dirt into the wounds. As the victim pulled himself up and down on the cross to breathe, the dirt acted like sandpaper and kept blood flowing out of the back and down the cross.

The severity of the beatings is emphasized by the fact that Jesus could not carry his cross to Calvary, but He had to be helped by Simon of Cyrene. It is an erroneous belief that Jesus carried the "T" shaped instrument of His death through the streets of Jerusalem. He probably only carried the horizontal piece, which was set into a hewn-out crotch of a vertical, permanently implanted stake at the crucifixion site. The horizontal piece, between five and six feet long, probably weighed from seventy to one hundred pounds, yet Jesus was so weakened by the beatings, He could not even carry it the relatively short distance to Golgatha.

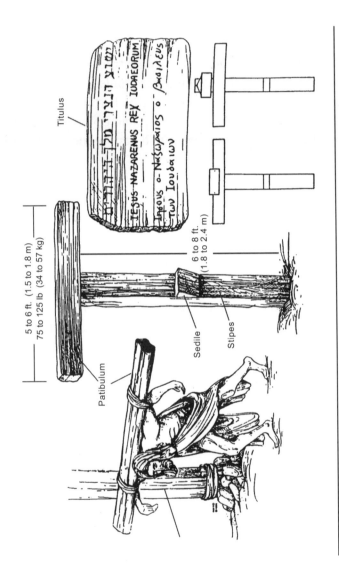

Cross and titulus. Left, Victim carrying crossbar (patibulum) to site of upright post (stipes). Center, Low Tau cross (crux commissa), commonly used by Romans at time of Christ. Upper right, Rendition of Jesus' titulus, with name and crime—Jesus of Nazareth, King of the Jews—written in Hebrew, Latin, and Greek. Lower right, Possible methods for attaching titulus to Tau cross (left) and Latin cross (right).

(This chart courtesy of the *Journal of the American Medical Association*, March 21, 1986, Vol. 255, No. 11, "On the Physical Death of Jesus Christ," pp. 1455–1463.)

The Anatomy of the Crucifixion

When the hands were pierced with approximately seven-inch-long spikes, they were strategically placed in the wrist. (Traditionally, we have accepted the notion that the nails were driven through the palms of the hands. That location, however, would not support the weight of the body.) The spike was driven into the wrist where it severed the median nerve. The hand immediately retracted into a claw. The prophecy of the crucifixion in Psalm 22 says in verse 17 that He could see His bones. This means that as the weight of His body was supported by the nails, when Jesus pulled himself up to breathe, the holes became so large He could look across at His wrists and actually see the bones.

The median nerve is the nerve of the "funny bone." If it were in fact severed in both wrists, shooting pains would have arced across Jesus' heart each time it beat. These impulses greatly weakened the heart. Psalm 22 refers to this too.

> *I am poured out like water, and all my bones [shoul-*
> *der joints] are out of joint: my heart is like wax; it is*
> *melted in the midst of my bowels.*
>
> *Psalm 22:14*

Jesus' feet were nailed to the cross probably between the second and third metatarsal bones. This is a crucial pressure point—just pressing upon it with your finger can send shivers up your spine. Whether there was one nail for both of His feet or a nail for each foot is not known. Regardless, Jesus' feet were nailed with a slight bend in the knee to allow Him to stand up and breathe. The nail wound itself was enough to cause Jesus to go into shock, let alone the fact that He had to stand on it.

There is good reason to believe that Jesus was nailed to a low "tau" (T–shaped) cross instead of being from ten to thirteen feet in the air. The Bible states in John 19:29 that Jesus was offered a drink with a sponge upon a hyssop stalk. The hyssop plant typically is no longer than twenty-four inches. Combining this length with the average arm's length of a soldier, we can conclude that Jesus was only about seven or eight feet off the ground. This means that the

Lord was executed at "eye-level" with mankind, not high above the crowd in a "distant" fashion.

The severity of blood loss, due primarily to the wounds on His back, is what caused our Lord to say, "I thirst." As the blood loss continued, Jesus' body began to extract any and all of His fluids in order to make more blood. Verse 15 of Psalm 22 states that His tongue cleaved to the roof of His mouth. His thirst must have been beyond anything we could imagine.

Finally, a spear pierced Jesus' side (John 19:34). The word for "side" in the Greek text is *pleura*. *Pleura* is the name of the lining for the lungs and other related items in the thoracic, or chest area. The spear lunge was a pinpointed thrust that most likely entered between the rib bones, where it pierced the heart. The water that came out with the blood was from the ruptured pulmonary sac that surrounds the heart. Filled with fluid, this sac acts as a cushion to protect the heart from any outside wounds, or from any excess pounding as a result of trying to move less and less blood through the body. This is what Jesus' heart must have experienced.

The pictures we see of Jesus hanging on the cross are white-washed and cleaned up because we do not want to deal with the reality of what He actually went through. The actual fact is that the cross was an ugly, bloody place. A human body holds approximately five units of blood and Jesus shed *all* of His blood for our redemption. Jesus' hair was matted down from the blood from the crown of thorns. There were bruises all about His face, and blood from the wounds of His beatings and scourging streamed down His chest and His arms and His wrists. The vertical cross member was soaked with the blood that ran out of His back.

As Jesus endured all this pain, He was as silent as a lamb before its shearer. He received the cruelest execution ever known to exist. It was not the nails that kept Him on the cross—it was His love for the people of the world. God, His Father, would have delivered Him at the hand of twelve legions of angels (Matthew 26:53), but Jesus made His choice and took the pain.

Not only did He take all this pain, but He also hung naked upon the cross to cover our shame. Hebrews 12:2 says that Jesus endured the cross but He despised the shame. He hung on a cross outside Jerusalem during a high and holy feast that every male Jew in the world was required to attend. He was reviled by onlookers as they made their way into the city for the evening sacrifice of the Passover. Little did most of them know that they were walking by the Lamb of God, who takes away the sins of the world. Jesus was made a public spectacle for the furtive shame of our secret sins.

The sacrifice that Jesus made on the cross for our redemption is God's legal payment to reconcile us back to Him. As we study the seven ways that Jesus bled, let us remember the details of His death and commit ourselves in faith not to pay the devil again for what Jesus has already purchased. Let us fully receive and appreciate the payment that was made to redeem us and bring us into God's favor and the blessings of our blood-bought covenant.

Seven Ways Jesus Bled

- Out of His hands
- Out of His feet
- Out of His back
- Out of His crown
- Out of His side
- Out of His brow
- He was bruised

Chapter 5

Seven Ways Jesus Bled

The blood of Jesus is the most precious, life-giving substance ever known to the world. By accepting it as a sacrifice, we receive eternal life, health, prosperity, and peace. For those who reject it, the sentence of death, damnation, and separation from God ensues. Christians who apply His blood properly find peace and fellowship with God, but if they take it for granted and count it as a common thing, they are nigh unto being cursed (Hebrews 6:6, 10:29). The benefits received from knowing about the blood are commensurate with the consequences of ignorance or denial. It was shed so that God could demonstrate His love and mercy. Those who reject it will feel God's wrath and fury.

Before we begin exploring the seven different ways that Jesus bled, we need to examine some background details that provide additional meaning and depth to our understanding. We have already seen the profile of the seven bleedings from Leviticus 16:14, but there is another section of Scripture that illustrates this, too. It is found in Isaiah 53:4–6.

> *Surely he hath borne our griefs, and carried our sorrows [in the Garden of Gethsemane when he bled out of His brow]: yet we did esteem him stricken, smitten of God, and afflicted. But he was wounded*

> *[in His hands, feet, crown and side] for our trans-*
> *gressions, he was bruised for our iniquities [by the*
> *beatings]: the chastisement of our peace was upon*
> *him; and with his stripes [on His back] we are*
> *healed. All we like sheep have gone astray; we have*
> *turned every one to his own way [by the way we*
> *have walked with our feet]; and the LORD hath laid*
> *on him the iniquity of us all.*
>
> *Isaiah 53:4–6*

This section of Scripture contains a great truth that is hidden just beneath the surface. Not only does it profile the seven ways Jesus bled, it also underscores the importance of the cross and redemption. The book of Isaiah is a paradigm of the Word of God. It has sixty-six chapters, which corresponds to the sixty-six books of the Bible. The major breaking point of structure is between chapters 39 and 40. This relates to the division between the Old Testament and the New Testament. In the last twenty-seven chapters, the same number of books in the New Testament, there are three sections. In the middle of the middle section is Isaiah 53. In the middle of that section is the portion describing the redemption of the cross and the ways that Jesus bled. God has concealed a precious truth here we can now search out (Proverbs 25:2).

By putting this statement exactly in the middle, of the middle, of the middle of the New Testament profile in Isaiah, God is directing us to the central focal point of New Testament truth—the cross and our redemption. God shows us the seven ways that Jesus bled for our redemption in the middle verses of this section.

When we couple this understanding with the profile of the Day of Atonement, the most holy day of the Jewish year, we can deduce that we are dealing with a magnificent truth that God has hidden for those who have eyes to see and ears to hear. This is a revelation of highest magnitude and importance of understanding.

From Leviticus, we learned the profile of the seven ways the Lord bled.

And he shall take of the blood of the bullock, and sprinkle it with his finger upon the mercy seat east-ward; and before the mercy seat shall he sprinkle of the blood with his finger seven times.

Leviticus 16:14

The number seven has scriptural significance; it means spiritual perfection and covenant order. There are thirty-three usages of "seven times" in the Bible, ranging from the ways Jesus bled to purifying the leper, to forgiving someone seventy times seven. This shows the "perfect" way God would have something done. The reference to the blood being sprinkled seven times before the mercy seat demonstrates the total redemption available to us illustrated in the book of Hebrews.

*Let us draw near with a true heart in full assurance of faith, having our hearts **sprinkled** from an evil conscience, and our bodies washed with pure water.*

Hebrews 10:22

The sprinkling of the blood before the mercy seat exemplifies the offering of redemption and salvation and also the cleansing of the evil conscience. References to sprinkling are seen throughout the book of Hebrews, and in 1 Peter 1:2.

*Elect according to the foreknowledge of God the Father, through sanctification of the Spirit, unto obedience and **sprinkling** [applying] of the blood of Jesus Christ: Grace unto you, and peace, be multiplied.*

1 Peter 1:2

We see that Jesus' blood was shed for us to be cleansed, therefore we can also enter with Him into God's presence. This was typified by the blood of the goat in Leviticus 16:15. Jesus bled so He could enter into the presence of God and take us with Him. It is only by His blood we are allowed to enter.

PERFECT REDEMPTION

> *Jesus saith unto him, I am the way, the truth, and the*
> *life: no man cometh unto the Father, but by me.*
> *John 14:6*

Each way Jesus bled has a significant type of forgiveness that God extends to mankind. All of these ways are specifically applied so we can enter into the presence of God and have fellowship with Him. The blood that came out of Jesus' hands, for example, forgives the kinds of sins, iniquities, and transgressions our hands may commit. The blood that came out of His crown, however, forgives us in a different, yet equally important way. It forgives us for any mental anxiety we may experience. When the blood of Jesus is fully applied, a complete and perfect forgiveness before the Father fills the heart of every believer. Then, as the feast day foretold and fulfilled, atonement, or "perfect redemption" is received.

In addition to Jesus' blood being shed to forgive our sins, iniquities, and transgressions, it also redeems us from curses that potentially have been working in our lives. Galatians 3:13 tells us that we were redeemed from the curse of the law when the Lord hung on the tree. The curse on the hands has been turned into a blessing because the Lord loves you. Likewise, the curse on the crown now has been changed to an asset instead of a liability. The blood that came out of His feet breaks the curse of walking the wrong way and making wrong decisions, and the blood that came out of His brow breaks the curse of being weak-willed and weak-minded.

Deuteronomy 23:5 explains why these curses become blessings—because God loves us.

> *But the LORD thy God turned the curse into a bless-*
> *ing unto thee, **because the LORD thy God loved***
> ***thee.***
> *Deuteronomy 23:5b*

It is very important to remember *all* the ways Jesus bled so that we can apply His blood to these areas. It is not only cleansing and refreshing, but also spiritually renewing. As individuals properly apply His blood and the curses are reversed, weaknesses become strengths. For example, once the blood that came out of Jesus' brow is understood and applied, a person can then be confident and committed, instead of being weak willed and full of fear.

Most Christians are familiar with the different ways that Jesus bled. Can you recite them from memory? Stop now and see if you can.

After teaching on the subject many times and asking people to try to remember the ways Jesus bled, I have found a very interesting fact. Hardly anyone remembers all seven places. Even more revealing is that the two places most commonly missed are the last places where the blood is applied, and where Christians continue to suffer the most pain and lack of deliverance. Did you remember all seven ways? This may reveal vital information to you concerning your spiritual state and where you need to focus your application of the blood.

Let me ask you again to stop and try to recall the ways that Jesus bled for you. Write them down. There could be a great revelation in this for you and an indicator for deliverance.

The first place people usually remember where Jesus bled is out of His hands, and then out of His feet. Then, they remember His side, His crown, and His back. These are the locations where the bleeding was most obvious. (Was this true of your recollection?) The last two places people remember where He bled are the ones that potentially could have caused Jesus the most agony and internal pain. Jesus bled out of His brow, and He was bruised internally. These were places that were unseen, and likewise, they are the "unseen" places in peoples' lives that continually cause torment.

As we study the ways Jesus bled, we will learn certain truths regarding bleeding from several verses of Scripture. We will also learn the significance of a particular way Jesus bled by simply recognizing the place where His blood came out; i.e., out of His hands for the deeds we have done.

If we approached this inquiry by chronologically examining the ways Jesus bled, we would see that the first two ways He bled was to clean us up on the inside. (These are usually the last two places where the blood is applied.) This revelation emphasizes that God is more concerned about us being clean on the inside than on the outside (Matthew 23:27–28). We also will realize that the last way He bled, out of His side for our transgressions, was to forgive the first transgression ever committed. Only then can we say what Jesus said, "It is finished."

We are going to cover the ways that Jesus bled for inward cleansing (out of His brow and bruised for our iniquities) last because this will dovetail into the section dealing with iniquity. The understanding of iniquity is perhaps the least examined truth of all the important foundational issues in a Christian's life. Victory over iniquity will free victims from life-long struggles. My decision for the order of covering these seven ways was not just arbitrarily made for this reason, either. I have discovered that these two ways (out of the brow and bruising) among all seven, hold the most deliverance for people.

Before beginning, however, it will benefit you to know one more interesting note regarding the ways Jesus bled. I have said that Jesus bled seven ways, but more accurately, I should say, "He bled seven ways *for our redemption.*" Jesus bled another way long before He started his ascent to Calvary. Can you think how?

Jesus bled at circumcision when He was eight days old (Leviticus 12:3; Philippians 3:5; Luke 1:59). The number eight, for the eighth way Jesus bled, is scripturally significant of a new beginning.[8] The significance of circumcision for Israel was to enter into the covenant blessing of Abraham. We now learn that Jesus bled at His circumcision in order that the Gentiles may also enter into the covenant blessing of Abraham.

Also, in regard to other ways that Jesus bled, some have also suggested that Jesus bled out of His face when his beard was plucked out during the ridicules and beatings. This was prophesied in Isaiah 50:6 and, no doubt, was done. But blood is not necessarily shed when hairs are pulled out of the follicles. Furthermore, the gospels do not record this event. Nonetheless, just to be thorough, if this was one of the ways Jesus bled, it would have been during the time of the mockings and beatings. It would then represent the forgiveness of the sins, iniquities, and transgressions of the priesthood and/or church leaders, since the beard was specifically indicative of the priesthood (Psalm 133:2).

We are going to cover the seven ways Jesus bled that Scripture verifies, and we will cover these in the order that is most commonly remembered: (1) He bled out of His hands, (2) He bled out of His feet, (3) He bled out of His back, (4) He bled out His side, (5) He bled out of His crown, (6) He bled out of His brow, and (7) He bled when He was bruised.

As we study each of these ways, I pray for the Holy Spirit to convict you of unconfessed sin, iniquity, and transgression in your life. John 16:7–9 says that the Holy Spirit was sent for this purpose. My prayer is not for condemnation, but for conviction—to the end of confession and cleansing. When we move on toward the end of the book, we will take the information that is shared here and employ it practically by applying Jesus' shed blood. It may benefit you to write down those things the Holy Spirit reveals to you as you read the different ways that Jesus bled.

We will discover the kinds of sins, iniquities, and transgressions that are revealed and also the curses that were broken. We will also see the strength His blood now yields to those who apply it and live in its power.

Holy Spirit, I ask in the name of Jesus Christ that You move within Your people. Search their hearts and bring things back to their remembrance. Jesus sent You as our Helper. Help each and every person to recall areas and incidents that have kept them separated from God. We need Your help, Holy Spirit, to understand why the

blood was shed and where and how to apply it. We thank You for Your faithfulness, in the name of Jesus Christ.

He Bled Out of His Hands

The first usage of blood in the Bible deals with the blood of Abel that cries out to God. That blood was shed by the hands of Cain.

> *And now art thou cursed from the earth, which hath opened her mouth to receive thy brother's blood from thy hand.*
>
> *Genesis 4:11*

This verse shows that the hands of a man or woman are the instruments of work. Cain's hands were cursed by committing murder. The blood of Abel stained his hands: only the blood of Jesus can remove the stain.

When the seven-inch long spikes pierced the hands of our Lord Jesus Christ, the most precious, versatile, and gifted instruments of construction were destroyed. His hands were the very instruments of God incarnate. They handled the Word of God with more grace and truth than anyone who came before or after. Jesus laid His hands on the sick and they recovered. He laid His hands on the disciples and ordained them. With His hands, He overturned tables in the temple; He raised up Jairus' daughter; and He fed the hungry multitudes with fish and bread.

His pure hands were given as a sacrifice to cleanse the world of their evil deeds.

The book of James shows the correlation between the hands and the heart of man. What the heart can conceive, the hands can achieve.

> *Draw nigh to God, and he will draw nigh to you. Cleanse your hands, ye sinners; and purify your hearts, ye double minded.*   *James 4:8*

It was with her hands that Eve partook of the forbidden fruit. It was with his hands that Adam took the fruit when she gave it to him. The problem was not with the hands, but with a heart that made the decision to put them to work. Jesus gave His hands, and the blood that came out of them, for the forgiveness of everything Adam and Eve had done. Jesus, likewise, gave His hands in sacrifice for everything your hands have done.

Look at your hands and ask yourself this question—what have they done? When I look at mine, I think about the bottles of beer they have handled in years past and the immoral acts they have committed. They are stained with sins. What can wash away my sin? Nothing but the blood of Jesus.

The blood that came out of Jesus' hands was shed in the exact place that God foreordained it. God knew that our hands would be stained with sins, transgressions, and iniquities, and that these were going to be open debts before Him.

The actual point where the spikes of the nails entered was not in the palms of Jesus' hands (as some have presumed), but at the base of them—at the junction of the wrist and the hand. (We know this from exhumed corpses of crucified victims from this era.) When the spike entered, it did not break any bones, but severed the median nerve that runs the length of the arm, underneath the shoulder, across the chest, and arcs across the heart. Have you ever hit your "funny bone" and felt the pain shoot up your arm? This is what Jesus endured so that the curse of sins, iniquities, and transgressions could be taken off of your hands and out of your heart.

A chart on the following page illustrates the placement of nails in Jesus' wrists.

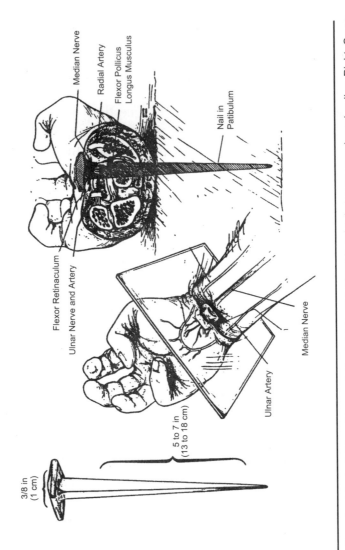

Median Nerve

Radial Artery

Flexor Pollicus Longus Musculus

Nail in Patibulum

Flexor Retinaculum

Ulnar Nerve and Artery

Median Nerve

Ulnar Artery

5 to 7 in (13 to 18 cm)

3/8 in (1 cm)

Nailing of wrists. Left, Size of iron nail. Center, Location of nail in wrist, between carpals and radius. Right, Cross section of wrist, at level of plane indicated at left, showing path of nail, with probable transection of median nerve and impalement of flexor pollicis longus, but without injury to major arterial trunks and without fractures of bones.

(This chart courtesy of the *Journal of the American Medical Association*, March 21, 1986, Vol. 255, No. 11, "On the Physical Death of Jesus Christ," pp. 1455–1463.)

If you squeeze your wrist, you can see your fingers draw up into a claw. This is what happened to Jesus. These beautiful hands and instruments of God were drawn up into a claw. Psalm 22 illustrates what happened. Jesus could look at His wrists and see the bones through the holes the spikes made.

> *I may tell all my bones: they look and stare upon me.*
> *Psalm 22:17*

The weight of His body upon the nails was so great that it pulled His shoulders out of joint, too.

> *I am poured out like water, and all my bones are out*
> *of joint: my heart is like wax; it is melted in the*
> *midst of my bowels.*
> *Psalm 22:14*

Jesus bled for the curse of sins, iniquities, and transgressions to be removed from our hands. The remedy for haunting memories is choosing to dwell on the memory of His pain rather than memories of our own evil actions. When these memories come to your mind, recall the gaping holes in His wrists and the blood that ran down His arms. Recall the severed median nerve pulsating across Jesus' chest like electrical currents jolting His heart with every throbbing beat. Jesus paid for your forgiveness. Take it by faith—faith in the blood.

By His blood, the curse of sin has been removed from your hands. Now you can lay hands on the sick and they will recover, because—by the supreme act of God—the Holy Spirit can flow through your spiritually purified hands.

I mentioned, when looking at my hands, that I remembered beer bottles and immoral acts I had committed. Jesus not only paid for those acts to be forgiven, but for the curse to be broken. Now when I look at my hands, I think about the number of sick people made well by the Holy Spirit using them (as opposed to me abusing them). Now I think about the number of pages my hands have turned in the Bible, or the lines of type they have written. They are now the instruments of righteousness, not unrighteousness. The same is true of your hands. By the blood of Jesus that came out of His hands, the curse of sin, iniquity, and transgression has been broken off of your hands. We are thankful for His mercy. Now, the exhortation from Romans 6:13 should continually echo in our hearts and minds.

> *Neither yield ye your members as instruments of unrighteousness unto sin: but yield yourselves unto God, as those that are alive from the dead, and your members as instruments of righteousness unto God.*
> *Romans 6:13*

The blood that came out of His hands was shed for the forgiveness of every willful wrong act you have ever committed and His blood has turned your hands into instruments of righteousness unto God. The blood that came out of Jesus' hands did not just cancel the curse—it reversed the curse and turned it into a blessing. Now, your hands are instruments of righteousness. You should decide to never use your hands for any immoral or sinful act again. Dedicate them to the work of God and realize that they are the most intricate devices by which you can do the works of God.

He Bled Out of His Feet

Can you imagine the point of a spike being specifically positioned on the top of your foot? Can you imagine a man holding a mallet ready to drive that spike directly through your foot? Think about the impact of the mallet. When it happened to Jesus, the first blow drove the spike through his foot. The second scarcely imbedded it in the cross. It must have taken four or five or six blows to sufficiently sink that spike deep into the wooden cross.

The spike that was driven into the feet of the Lord was probably placed between the second and third metatarsal bones. It is a place so tender that it pains us to just to push upon it with our fingers. Jesus bore the weight of His *whole body* on this spike. He had to stand up on this nail and pull Himself up with the nails in his wrists in order to breathe and in order to speak so that He could relieve the pressure of the rope about His waist. Can you imagine the pain?

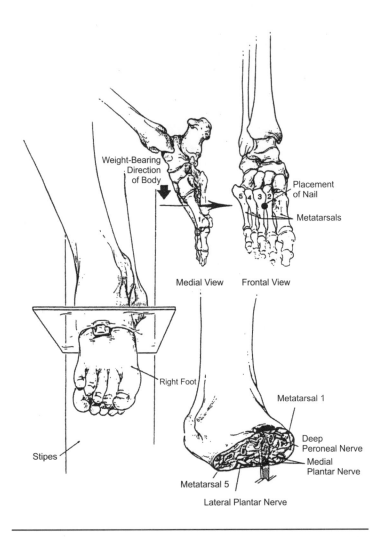

Nailing of feet. Left, Position of feet atop one another and against stipes. Upper right, Location of nail in second intermetatarsal space. Lower right, Cross section of foot, at plane indicated at left, showing path of nail.

(This chart courtesy of the *Journal of the American Medical Association*, March 21, 1986, Vol. 255, No. 11, "On the Physical Death of Jesus Christ," pp. 1455–1463.)

Why did God choose to have Jesus bleed out of His feet? What is He trying to show us? When we consider the feet of a man we understand that they relate to the way he walks, the direction he takes, and therefore the decisions he makes. The steps he takes with his feet dictate the direction of his life. We have all experienced the futility of making our own decisions and walking in our own ways.

> *O LORD, I know that the way of man is not in him-self: it is not in man that walketh to direct his steps.*
> *Jeremiah 10:23*

When the spike that pierced Jesus' foot was placed between His bones and the force of the mallet drove the nail through His flesh, blood spurted out of the hole. That blood was shed for all the wrong ways we have walked—all the wrong decisions we have made and wrong paths we have traveled upon.

> *All we like sheep have gone astray; we have turned every one to **his own way**; and the LORD hath laid on him the iniquity of us all.*
> *Isaiah 53:6*

Notice Isaiah 53:6 says that the Lord laid this iniquity on Him. Many times we have generational patterns (see chapter 7) within us that cause us to walk in the paths that we do. Bad decisions are repeatedly made because of the iniquity in our lives. A lady came to me awhile back and said, "I always fall for the wrong guy. I've been married three times and every man I have married has been a jerk." I looked at her and said, "Ma'am, the problem is not the men, but the iniquity that drives you to make the wrong decisions time and time again."

Worry, lust, anger, self-consciousness, and all other causes of our continual bad decisions were all nailed to the cross. When we went down the wrong road with the wrong person at the wrong time, when we made bad decisions that cost us years of our commitment to the Lord, the blood from His feet was shed for this iniquity to be forgiven.

PERFECT REDEMPTION

Perhaps the most easily recognized wrong decision we ever make occurs when we walk in our own ways. Even when we forsake the commandment of God by transgression and "do our own thing," the blood out of Jesus' feet was shed to forgive us of those wrongs, too. What the hands represent to the action, the feet represent to the decision behind the action. Job 31:6 and 7 illustrate the decision, the motive, and the action.

> *Let me be weighed in an even balance, that God may know mine integrity. If my step [decision] hath turned out of the way, and mine heart [motive] walked after mine eyes, and if any blot hath cleaved to mine hands [action];*
>
> *Job 31:6–7*

Praise the Lord for forgiveness from making wrong decisions. Wrong decisions are the root of guilt. When the sin, iniquity, and transgression is forgiven, the guilt leaves, too. Guilt is covered by the blood of Jesus that came out of His feet.

In a class I was teaching, a woman came to me and said, "I married the wrong man. Am I forgiven for this, too?" I could see by the Holy Spirit there was a hidden motive behind her question. I answered her by saying, "Yes, you are forgiven for the sin of the decision, but the consequence is not the same thing. You are obligated to live with him according to the Word of God in 1 Corinthians 7:10–13." I also told her, "The wrong is forgiven, and now the same Lord who forgave you will give you the strength and wisdom to deal with the consequences."

Likewise, years ago, a young teen–age girl came to me and told me she was pregnant out of wedlock. She asked me to pray for her. When I finished, she asked, "Is it gone now?" I explained the same thing to her. God not only forgives the action, but He will also help you to live with the consequences, but they are not the same.

The mercy of God is from everlasting to everlasting. He loves to show mercy and for that reason the blood of Jesus was shed out of

His feet to forgive our wrong decisions. Not only was His blood shed to forgive our wrong decisions, but also to help strengthen us to make the right ones. The Lord can now direct our ways through the Holy Spirit so we are able to receive the spirit of wisdom.

> *I have taught thee in the way of wisdom; I have led thee in right paths. When thou goest, thy steps shall not be straitened; and when thou runnest, thou shalt not stumble.*
>
> *Proverbs 4:11–12*

> *That the God of our Lord Jesus Christ, the Father of glory, may give unto you the spirit of wisdom and revelation in the knowledge of him.*
>
> *Ephesians 1:17*

We can claim the New Testament reality of having the curse reversed instead of walking in the shadow of wrong decisions. Now, we can walk in confidence of the Holy Spirit to lead us into proper decisions because we have the Counselor living inside us. The blood of Jesus was shed out of His feet for the forgiveness of walking in the wrong ways and making wrong decisions. When the blood is properly applied, it reverses the curse and turns it into a blessing—the blessing of being able to walk in spiritual wisdom as we are led by the Holy Spirit.

He Bled Out of His Back

Immediately after the mock trial before Pontius Pilate, Jesus was delivered to the Roman soldiers to be scourged.

> *And so Pilate, willing to content the people, released Barabbas unto them, and delivered Jesus, **when he had scourged him**, to be crucified.*
>
> *Mark 15:15*

PERFECT REDEMPTION

Scourging means to be beaten with a whip. The whips had small pieces of bone or metal woven into the tip of the strands. These whips did not just cut, but ripped, shredded, and gouged as they lacerated the flesh. Every time the whip ripped across His flesh, Jesus became our substitute. As mentioned in the previous chapter, some have thought that Jesus was beaten with thirty-nine lashes. The Romans, however, were the ones inflicting the torture and they beat Him—without regard to Jewish law—almost to death.

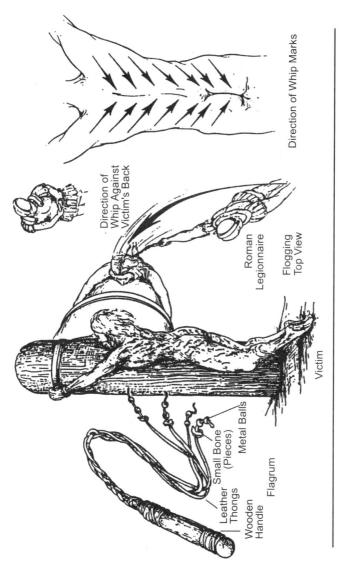

Direction of Whip Marks

Direction of Whip Against Victim's Back

Roman Legionnaire

Flogging Top View

Victim

Leather Thongs

Small Bone (Pieces)

Metal Balls

Wooden Handle

Flagrum

Scourging. Left, Short whip (flagrum) with lead balls and sheep bones tied into leather thongs. Center left, Naked victim tied to flogging post. Deep stripelike lacerations were usually associated with considerable blood loss. Center right, View from above, showing position of lictors. Right, Inferomedial direction of wounds.

(This chart courtesy of the *Journal of the American Medical Association*, March 21, 1986, Vol. 255, No. 11, "On the Physical Death of Jesus Christ," pp. 1455–1463.)

PERFECT REDEMPTION

The fact that Jesus was whipped on His back is very significant. The back is the strongest part of the physical body, but it is also defenseless. Jesus gave His back—His strength, so that He could be our strength when we are weak. He became defenseless so He could defend us against an unseen enemy.

The verse of Scripture in Isaiah 53:5 gives the reason why Jesus had to bleed out of his back: for our healing.

> *But he was wounded for our transgressions, he was bruised for our iniquities: the chastisement of our peace was upon him; **and with his stripes we are healed**.*   *Isaiah 53:5*

When we are sick and have no strength—He is not only our healing, but also our strength. When it seems we are defenseless, He is our defense. The debilitation of sickness and weakness will come upon you at one time or another. Jesus bled for your healing. He also bled so that you could be strong in Him when those times come.

1 Peter 2:24 reveals the New Testament fulfillment of this Old Testament prophecy.

> *Who his own self bare our sins in his own body on the tree, that we, being dead to sins, should live unto righteousness**: by whose stripes ye were healed***
> *1 Peter 2:24*

The stripes on His back and the blood that came out of these stripes accomplished our healing. There is healing in the blood of Jesus. He shed His blood so that we could enter into a covenant with God and have the legal right to claim our health. Hebrews 10:19–23 gives us the details of our rights and faith for healing.

> *Therefore, brethren, **having boldness to enter the Holiest by the blood of Jesus**, by a new and living way which He consecrated for us, through the veil, that is, **His flesh**, and having a High Priest over the*

*house of God, let us draw near with a true heart in full assurance of faith, having our hearts sprinkled from an evil conscience and our bodies washed with pure water. **Let us hold fast the confession** of our hope without wavering, **for He who promised is faithful**.*

Hebrews 10:19–23 NKJ

In the Old Testament covenant there was a provision for healing through the blood of the Passover lamb profiling our New Covenant reality. Psalm 105:37 confirms there was not one feeble person among the estimated two and a half million Israelites.

Another account of healing for the people is documented in 2 Chronicles 30:20.[9]

When we think about the cruel beating our Lord took for us, we should become righteously indignant regarding our healing. This is the testimony of the Word of God and we should hold fast to our confession. The blood of Jesus has been shed so that we can claim our healing in the covenant we have with our Father God.

The best time to claim our healing is before we are sick, and not to take the sickness when it tries to come to us. What would you do if a delivery person knocked on your door and handed you a package you did not order? Would you take it? What if he was dressed in a red suit and had a pitchfork, horns, and a curly tail? What if you looked at the return address and it said, "From the devil, Flame Avenue, Fiery Pit, Hell, Zip code 666?" Would you still take it? I don't think so, and yet this is what we do when the devil tries to stick us with a sickness. When you confess, "Oh my, I have a cold," you have signed the delivery receipt. Or when you say, "I'm coming down with this or that," you just opened the door for him to bring it in.

Do not confess the symptoms, but instead call the devil a liar and tell him to take his delivery back where he came from. Not confessing these symptoms is not denial, it is faith in what is not seen.

PERFECT REDEMPTION

Faith is confessing health in the presence of symptoms. Hold fast to the confession of your faith and do not take the package. Return to sender.

It is not an uncommon truth that Jesus bled out of His back for our healing, but there is a related truth we must cover too. This deals with *what* the blood that came out of His back forgives us for. We have seen that the blood that came out of His hands forgives us for what we have done with our hands, and the blood that came out of His feet forgives us for the wrong decisions we have made. But the blood that came out of His back also avails forgiveness: for the sins we have committed against our bodies.

Our bodies are the temple of the Holy Spirit, and as such we should be, and should have been, treating them with respect and holiness. The Word of God tells us in 2 Corinthians 7:1 that we should perfect holiness in our flesh as well as in our spirit. All of us have sinned against our bodies—whether it has been overeating as in the sin of gluttony, or being tattooed as in the sin of marking our bodies—which belong to God. Many of us are receiving the consequences of such sins. The good news is that the blood of Jesus that came out of His back was shed so that we could be forgiven of these sins.

Just as the sins of lying or adultery can be forgiven, sins against the body can be forgiven also. If the truth is known, what prevents people from receiving healing more than anything else is condemnation resulting from sins we have committed. That is why Jesus said to the paralyzed man, "Thy sins be forgiven thee," in Matthew 9:2. When we realize that the sins we have committed against our bodies can be forgiven, it will open new doors of faith for healing.

Yes, it is a sin to overeat. Likewise, it is a sin to drink alcohol—especially in excess. But if you do not apply the blood that came out of Jesus' back for forgiveness, the faith to be healed will likely never come. God restores to us the years of the cankerworm (Joel 2:25), which means that He can restore what we have lost. This applies to the sins we have sinned against our bodies. Just ask the

Lord to forgive you and, like you would for sins you have committed in your soul, repent and "come apart from the accursed thing." Likewise, repent and turn from the habits you have practiced that violate the sanctity of your body. Receive forgiveness and apply the blood of Jesus that came out of His back. By grace you are saved. By grace you are forgiven. By grace you are healed.

There is another truth regarding redemption and healing that is pertinent to our study. It comes from Romans 8:22 and 23.

> *For we know that the whole creation groans and labors with birth pangs together until now. And not only they, but we also who have the firstfruits of the Spirit, even we ourselves groan within ourselves, eagerly waiting for the adoption, **the redemption of our body**.*
>
> *Romans 8:22–23 NKJ*

The promise of this full and total redemption for our bodies is the resurrection. Verse 24 says that we are saved in this hope. That hope is the hope of a new resurrected body at the return of Jesus Christ (Philippians 3:21). Until then, we are going to labor and groan under the curse of corruption. God did not repeal the curse of the corruption of the flesh, but instead, overwrote it in hope of a new body.

There is a lesson of healing in the covenant we are now under. It is this: in this life, we are still going to suffer corruption, groaning, and travailing. God, however, promises us length of days, long life, health, and strength. Moses experienced this. He did not lose any of his natural forces or health (Deuteronomy 34:7) because he embraced the presence of God and the affairs of holiness within the covenant. We should take a stand on the covenant promise of being healed by His stripes and His blood. Jesus said continually, "Be it unto you according to your faith." If we have faith in the blood, God will reward us (Hebrews 11:6).

I heard someone say once, "The people who go to healing crusades are the ones who are not strong in their covenant with God." We praise God for any way He delivers healing to us, but most assuredly, healing by the blood of Jesus is a more fundamental right to a Christian for healing than any other means.

We can be strong in our bodies because we have the confidence to confess our healing. As the inevitable curse of corruption comes upon us, and our bodies begin to age and deteriorate, we can be strong in knowing that the redemption of our bodies at the resurrection is a surety, and we are saved in hope of the promise of a resurrected body.

By the blood that was shed out of His back, we have healing. The curse has been reversed. Now, we can be healthy.

He Bled Out of His Side

People often remember that Jesus bled out of His side because blood and water came out of this wound.

> *But one of the soldiers with a spear pierced his side,*
> *and forthwith came there out blood and water.*
> *John 19:34*

Chronologically, this is the last place Jesus bled because this was the last thing that had to be accomplished to redeem all of mankind, especially the transgression of Adam. This not only redeemed our transgressions, but the initial transgression of Adam as well. The fact that this verse says, "a spear pierced His side," parallels the verse in Isaiah 53:5, where it says, "But he was wounded for our transgressions." It literally means punctured or pierced. The truth is that Jesus was pierced for our transgressions.

We will discover in the next section of "Where the Blood Is Applied" that transgressions are intentional wrongs committed with full knowledge. Knowing the definition of transgression, as "an intentional wrong," gives us a greater appreciation for His bleeding. We shall see that it has a particular significance for Adam.

For years I wondered how water came out of Jesus' side. Then I discovered the word for "side" is the Greek word *pleura*. According to medical usage, the *pleura* is the membrane which lines the chest cavity and covers the lungs. This explanation means that Jesus was pierced in the chest, between the rib bones. In other words, the Roman soldier's spear most probably pierced His heart. The water that came out was the water in the sac that surrounded His heart. When the spear entered the heart, it ruptured this sac and both water and blood came out.

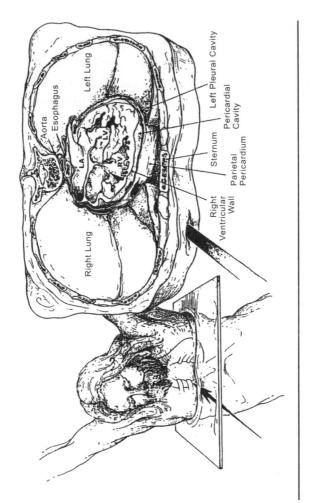

Spear wound to chest. Left, Probable path of spear. Right, Cross section of thorax, at level of plane indicated at left, showing structures perforated by spear. LA indicates left atruim; LV, left ventricle; RA, right atrium; RV, right ventricle.

(This chart courtesy of the *Journal of the American Medical Association*, March 21, 1986, Vol. 255, No. 11, "On the Physical Death of Jesus Christ," pp. 1455–1463.)

This sac, usually filled with serous fluid, enlarges when the heart is under serious strain. We can deduce that Jesus had lost a tremendous amount of blood from the previous loss of blood from His brow in the Garden of Gethsemane, from the crown of thorns on His head, from the scourging of His back, and from the nail wounds through His hands and feet. Logically, the reason for death could have been loss of blood and blood pressure. (This was the same cause of death for the Passover lamb.) Because we have the evidence of water coming out of His side, we now know that Jesus bled to death. He shed every bit of His blood to forgive all our transgressions.

Some Bible teachers have speculated that Jesus died of shock when He gave up the Holy Spirit. The fact is, He did not die of shock, but He died through obedience. Even though it was a great strain upon Him in an already greatly weakened state, Jesus still transacted the last portion of scriptural fulfillment when He asked for the wine and said, "I thirst." (See chapter 10, "The High Priest of Our Confession.") Jesus, through obedience, also died at the right time—3 P.M. This was the very same time for the evening sacrifice of the Passover lamb. Not only did Jesus die at the same time as the Passover lamb, but He also died in the same way—not of shock, but due to lack of blood pressure and loss of blood.

This shedding of Jesus' blood came directly out of His heart. The heart is not only used to signify the innermost part of our physical being, but also the innermost part of our spirit. In other words, the heart is the seat of our decision-making center. This fact reinforces that He was wounded for our transgressions—those times when we walk in rebellion to the commandments of God.

A transgression is a willing act of decision. It is not a sin of deception, but an error of intent, with full knowledge. The last way Jesus bled was for the most despicable act—disobeying God with full knowledge. His blood was shed for us to be forgiven when we willfully sin in our spiritual hearts.

Jesus Came to Redeem Adam

One aspect of the blood that came out of His side has impacted me more than anything else I have learned during my study of the blood of Jesus. This also deals with the fact that Jesus gave up the Holy Spirit before He died. We know this truth because He cried out, "Eli, Eli, lama sabachthani?" That is to say, "My God, My God, why have you forsaken me?" Jesus asked this question because God had put all the sins of the world on Him (2 Corinthians 5:21). He was smitten by God and afflicted (Isaiah 53:4). He was rejected by God so that He could redeem Adam, who rejected God.

The greater reality of what Jesus accomplished is hidden beneath the surface for those of us who have the heart to dig it out. The truth is that Jesus did not have to give up the Holy Spirit to redeem you or me because we never started with the Holy Spirit. Jesus had to give up the Holy Spirit to redeem not just *a* transgressor, but the *first* transgressor—Adam.

When John the Baptist said, "Behold! The Lamb of God, which taketh away the sin of the world," he was obviously referring to Jesus Christ. He did not say the sins, meaning every act, but sin (singular, emphasizing the whole complement, both root and fruit). Even though Jesus did bear the sins of each and every one of us, more specifically, He bore the sin of Adam—who caused death to be passed on to all men. Where was the sin of the world lying? The answer is directly on the stooped shoulders of Adam—the man who caused the whole world to sin.

> *Wherefore, as by one man [Adam] sin entered into the world, and death by sin; and so death passed upon all men, for that all have sinned.*
>
> *Romans 5:12*

From all of this information we can conclude that Jesus Christ left heaven and came to earth to redeem our great, great, great... grandfather, Adam. Jesus knew that if He could get Adam, in the process, He would get all of us, too. Jesus left the comfort of His Father's throne room and came to earth to be beaten, mocked, and rejected by the whole world in order to retrieve a transgressor who was suffering in hell.

Of all the people on earth, no one suffered like Adam. Likewise, no one on earth sinned the way Adam did. He was responsible for every sin, death, illness, broken relationship, and argument that ever took place. With full knowledge, he looked God in the face and gave away the rights to the planet. Not only that, but he gave it to God's archenemy. Adam carried the guilt of the whole human race. No one has ever hurt like Adam.

Once, when I was a boy, I committed a transgression. I was playing "Tarzan" with a couple of my friends in a tree house. We would swing from vines and ropes in the tree. I was standing on the limb above my friend with my hand on the rope at the same time he was ready to jump and grab the rope. I don't know what came over me—perhaps it was iniquity—but just as he jumped, I moved the rope. He fell down and when he hit the ground, a loud snap came from his leg. He began screaming, "My leg, my leg, I broke my leg." His leg was definitely broken, but more accurately, I broke his leg.

When his parents ran across the field, crying over him, I felt the guilt. When I saw them carry him off to the hospital, I felt the guilt. When I saw him walking around at school in a full-length leg cast, I felt the guilt. This, however, was nothing like what Adam felt. He felt that guilt and turmoil every time anything contrary to God's will happened to anyone.

Adam felt the sting of every sin, transgression, and iniquity in the world. How do you think he felt when Cain murdered Abel? The answer can be given in two words—guilty and responsible. How do you think Adam felt when the whole world was destroyed by water? The guilt was more than any other human can possibly imagine. Not only that, but Adam is responsible for it all. If anyone could have or even should have felt the guilt and responsibility of all the sin of the world, it was Adam. To go one step deeper, Adam did not even have an iniquity drive to compel him to transgress either. He did it "with his eyes wide open."

In my weakness, I have blamed Adam for many things and even used derogatory words about him. Not only has he been the most guilty and responsible man of the age, but also the most cursed. I heard one of my most favorite television personalities, John Hagee say "When I get to heaven, I'm going to give Adam a boot." I know how you feel Pastor Hagee, but Jesus did not give Adam a boot. He gave him a hand.

I have considered the possibility that the following incident may have happened in heaven.

The Father, Son, and Holy Spirit were looking down on the sons of men in Abraham's bosom—the section of hell where men had to stay until Jesus came to redeem them and take them to Paradise. They could see Adam's pain and torment. He was pacing around, wearing the guilt and responsibility of the whole world on his shoulders. Jesus looked at His Father and said, "I can't take it any longer. I'll go."

The Father hung His head. Tears filled His eyes. He said, "It's a big risk." Jesus said, "I know, but I'll do it." The Holy Spirit added, "I'll help." The Father said, "To get him, You'll have to legally go as the Second Adam." Jesus said, "I know." The Father said, "It will cost You Your life." Jesus said, "I know." The Father said, "Do You know what the devil will do to You?" "Yes," Jesus said, "I'll still go."

Perhaps we could understand someone giving his life to save a saint or an innocent child, but Jesus came to save a guilty traitor and murderer. When it was His time, He walked onto the scene and announced to Satan, who legally held Adam and all other Old Testament saints imprisoned, "I have come for Adam and his children." Satan replied, "It will cost you blood." Jesus acknowledged, "I know." And that was His last word. He went as a silent lamb— He never opened his mouth through all the torture. Jesus took the mental pressure, the beatings, the cruelty, the rejection, the whippings, the nails, the jeers, the thirst, the pain, and the shame. When He was hanging on the cross, Jesus had Adam and his children on his mind. It was love that kept Jesus there, not the nails.

The account of Jesus going into hell is described in the Gospel of Nicodemus,[10] an early first century apocryphal writing that many scholars attribute to Nicodemus. After storming the gates of hell (Psalm 86:13), guess who was the first person that Jesus retrieved? Adam! Jesus took him by the hand and delivered Adam, along with the other saints, to Paradise. Whether the Gospel of Nicodemus is apocryphal or not, it happened just the same.

The revelation that changed my life started with an understanding of the guilt and responsibility of Adam, but this is not where the revelation ended. I know now, beyond a shadow of a doubt, that my God and Father, My Lord Jesus, and the Holy Spirit love mercy. If anyone deserved to die and rot in hell, it was Adam—but God loves mercy. He wanted Adam reconciled, and He wants you and me reconciled to Him, too.

> *But God, who is rich in mercy, for his great love*
> *wherewith he loved us, Even when we were dead in*
> *sins, hath quickened us together with Christ, (by*
> *grace ye are saved;)*   *Ephesians 2:4–5*

Years ago, a man came to me and said he needed to confess a sin. I told him he had a priest and His name is Jesus. The man pressed the matter and insisted that he needed to tell someone. He confessed, "Some time ago, I needed some money to take a Bible class. I did not have the money, so I took a contract out on a man and murdered him for it." My poker face held, but my spirit man was writhing in pain. The man continued, "Do you think God can forgive me?" I thought about Adam and said, "Brother, God loves mercy. Jesus came to save someone with far greater guilt than yourself." I then added, "God can and does forgive you. Now the question is: can you forgive yourself?"

The last place that Jesus bled atoned for the first transgression ever committed. Neither you nor I have ever done anything to even rival the betrayal of Adam. Jesus not only forgave him, but came to earth to be brutalized for his redemption. Self-forgiveness can be a big problem (see chapter 13) but it can be overcome with the knowledge of how much our God loves us. God loves mercy and He wants you in His presence.

You may say, "You don't know how bad I have been." My response is, "You don't know how good God is."

When you get to this point, you need to be perfectly clear about accepting the substitution of Jesus' blood for your transgressions. Continuing to deny forgiveness is to reject atonement. Deal with yourself according to the revelation of the Word of God. Read a verse of the Bible. Believe it and get over the guilt. You have to manage your mind and your emotions.

Jesus bled and died for you. Take authority over the demon of self-pity and accept His forgiveness. Be an overcomer!

> *"Ye are of God, little children, and have overcome them: because greater is he that is in you, than he that is in the world."*
>
> *1 John 4:4*

The blood that Jesus shed out of His heart forgives you for rebellion. It was shed for you to be forgiven for the things you have done with full knowledge of them being wrong. Jesus bled for your forgiveness and also to reverse the curse of rebellion. Obedience is now the rule of your life. The blood that came out of His side has conquered rebellion.

He Bled Out of His Crown

Matthew 27:27 states that after the Roman soldiers beat Jesus, a whole band of soldiers stripped Him naked and mocked Him as a

King. They crowned Him with thorns.

> *Then the soldiers of the governor took Jesus into the*
> *common hall, and gathered unto him the whole band*
> *of soldiers. And they stripped him, and put on him a*
> *scarlet robe. And when they had platted **a crown of***
> ***thorns**, they put it upon his head, and a reed in his*
> *right hand: and they bowed the knee before him, and*
> *mocked him, saying, Hail, King of the Jews! And*
> *they spit upon him, and took the reed, and smote him*
> *on the head.*
>
> *Matthew 27:27–30*

Thorns grew out of the ground when God cursed it in Genesis 3:17–19. Isn't it interesting that the crown was made from the exact thing that grew from the cursed ground? Jesus bore the curse on the earth so that you could wear the crown of heaven (Revelation 4:4; 20:4). He bled so that you could reign.

While spending time in the woods recently, I found an Osage orange tree that has the longest thorns of any plant in North America. I wanted a crown of thorns to use while teaching *Perfect Redemption*, so I cut a number of long branches and began to make a crown of thorns. I twisted them together just as the Bible said. As I made it, I stopped to muse and said out loud, "What kind of demented madman could contrive such a horrible thing?" The answer is that it was contrived by a demon in a person wanting to mock the true King of Glory. And yet God, knowing in His foreknowledge that this would happen, prophesied it in the Scriptures (Leviticus 4:6, 17) as a foreshadowing of one of the seven sprinklings that the High Priest offered.

When the thorns pricked the crown of the Lord, the blood that He shed was for the forgiveness of those times we have made anything else but Jesus king in our lives. When someone makes something else "king" in his life, that something is placed ahead of God and takes the place of God in that person's life. Where the crown of thorns punctured Jesus' scalp was no mistake. He bled in this manner so that forgiveness can be given to all who apply His blood for committing the sin or transgression of idolatry.

The crown of man is composed primarily of the frontal lobe of the brain and the temple. The frontal lobe is the area of the brain, anatomically, that separates mankind from animals. This is where the true consciousness of man lies. The perimeter of the head where the crown lies is around the temple. It is no coincidence that this area is called the temple, because it very well could be the place most likely to house the Holy Spirit. When the blood of Jesus was shed from the crown, it covered mankind's sins, iniquities, and transgressions of having anything else more important than God. It purified the temple, the holiest of holy places.

Certainly, the shedding of Jesus' blood covers the sin of worshipping graven images, but idolatry is more than just that. It could be relationships with people, jobs, money, reputation, etc. Ezekiel 14 relates that idols may be set up in the heart.

> For every one of the house of Israel, or of the stranger that sojourneth in Israel, which separateth himself from me, and setteth up his **idols in his heart**, and putteth the stumblingblock of his iniquity before his face, and cometh to a prophet to enquire of him concerning me; I the LORD will answer him by myself:
>
> *Ezekiel 14:7*

Worshipping false gods was one of the Old Testament transgressions punishable by death. The blood of Jesus abolishes the iniquity relating to this sin or transgression. It infuriates God when His created beings worship anything but Him. The Apostle Paul's heart was stirred when he saw the whole city of Athens worshipping idols. I know how Paul felt. I have ministered in India and have seen people bowing down to idols. It makes me even more thankful for the blood of Jesus and for the mercy of God. He wants to forgive people.

The curse of idolatry is broken when the blood that came out of Jesus' crown is applied. When we apply this blood, we are able to coronate the Lord and give Him the proper place in our lives. The fulfillment of what Jesus did for us was to reinstate the regal position of mankind underneath God's sovereignty. Romans 5:17 shows us the true position.

> *For if by one man's offence death reigned by one; much more they which receive abundance of grace and of the gift of righteousness shall **reign in life by one, Jesus Christ**.*
>
> *Romans 5:17*

Chronologically, bleeding out of the crown was the fourth way Jesus bled. The number four is spiritually significant as the number of the world, i.e., four seasons, four points of the compass, the four horsemen of Revelation. This fourth occurrence bears a message too. Jesus is destined to be King of the world. He shed His blood so the world could be forgiven for rejecting Him, and so His chosen people could reign with Him in His Kingdom. Those who take up the cross and have fellowship with His sufferings will receive the blessings of rulership.

> *If we suffer, we shall also reign with him: if we deny him, he also will deny us.*
>
> *2 Timothy 2:12*

The blood that came out of His crown was shed for you to be crowned in glory. His crown was pierced with the curse of thorns so the curse on the ground can be lifted from you. When you apply the blood that came out of Jesus' crown, all idolatry can be removed. Now, instead of having something more important than Jesus, you can make Him King, and you can make your relationship with Him the most important thing in your entire life.

He Bled Out of His Brow

The first place Jesus bled for our redemption was out of His brow, but it is one of the last places that people remember.

> *And being in an agony he prayed more earnestly: and his sweat was as it were great drops of blood falling down to the ground.*
>
> Luke 22:44

The first way Jesus bled is of tremendous significance because it illustrates the first thing God wants. Jesus was laboring in prayer over the decision He had to make. Would He actually go through with the will of God and be obedient unto death? Verse 42 in Luke 22 reveals His struggle.

> *Saying, Father, if thou be willing, remove this cup from me: nevertheless not my will, but thine, be done.*
>
> Luke 22:42

Jesus was laboring over doing the will of God. He labored over this in prayer much the way we do when we are faced with a decision that threatens our comfort, the way we live, and even our life. When the blood came out of His brow, it was shed for us to be forgiven for those times we have been weak, full of fear, doubt, worry, or have even questioned the will of God.

Notice that Luke 22:44 says that it was the labor of prayer that caused Jesus to sweat blood. Not only did Jesus bleed for us to be forgiven for being weak in our minds, but He also bled for us to be forgiven when we do not pray as much as we should.

The accuracy of the Greek text says that His sweat "became" drops of blood. In other words, it started as sweat but turned into blood. This is exactly the description of a medical condition called hematidrosis[11] and it occurs under times of great mental stress and emotional trauma. The blood actually oozes out of the capillaries of the skin rather than the usual perspiration.

Jesus was agonizing over fulfilling the will of God. This was mental torment. He shed His blood for every fear, worry, and doubt you have ever had. "Surely He has borne our griefs and carried our sorrows" (Isaiah 53:4 NKJ). We have a High Priest who can be touched with the feeling of our infirmities (Hebrews 4:14–16). The Lord suffered through this agony so that He can sustain and strengthen us through all of our fears and doubts, even the fear of death (Hebrews 2:14–15). He became weak so we could be strengthened through Him.

It is quite significant that this happened in the Garden of Gethsemane while Jesus was alone (Luke 22:41). Mental unrest and disquietude is a lonely feeling and no one can see your pain. Many times this is the greatest pain anyone experiences and it goes on inside someone without anyone else noticing. We often hear testimonies of people being delivered from drug addiction or some form of lust. As great as these deliverances are, the pains of worry and fear present a different, and many times, greater obstacle to overcome.

Rest assured the Lord sees and knows your pain as He searches your heart through the Holy Spirit. He sees your inward pain and discomfort. His blood was shed out of His brow for you to be forgiven and to be strengthened through these trials.

When you agonize in fear of the future, or when you doubt you will have what you need to be able to do the will of God, or when you worry about how you will face a trying situation, remember the blood that came out of Jesus' brow. It was shed for your forgiveness, and also shed so that you can be strong instead of weak.

When the blood seeped out of the capillaries of His brow and fell to the ground, Jesus also broke the curse put on mankind when God said to Adam, "In the sweat of thy face, thou shalt eat bread."[12] The curse of laboring in our work is broken. We are now fulfilled in the laboring of our prayers. We still work, but now because of the curse being broken, the blessings of God in the covenant of Adam and Abraham are upon us. We are blessed in the field; we are blessed in the city; we are blessed in our rising; we are blessed in our sitting—in our comings and in our goings. These blessings are due to the blood of Jesus that was shed for us to be forgiven of the sins, iniquities, and transgressions of being weak in our minds.

This manner of Jesus' bleeding is rarely remembered because it represents the hidden secrets going on inside of our minds. The good news for people agonizing over being weak in their minds is that Jesus of Nazareth not only forgave the sin, iniquity, and transgression, but also paid the price for deliverance. I have had people say to me, "You just don't understand the pain I feel in my mind." Yes, that is true, I do not; but you have a High Priest Who does.

Have you ever perspired in prayer? Most people hardly ever perspire in praise and worship, much less in prayer. Even if you have, has it ever turned into blood?

Mental disease is a crippling killer because there *seems* to be no solution. Jesus is the answer. He not only understands it—He forgives it. He not only forgives it—He heals it. He not only heals it—He cures it and turns the curse into a blessing.[13] Where you have worried, now you can have trust. Where you have had fear, now you can have faith. Where you have had anxiety, now you can have rest in His arms.

All of this was paid for on Calvary; now you need to claim it and begin living it. When you apply the blood that was shed out of Jesus' brow, you can live free of mental weakness as you have faith in the blood that was shed for you.

He Was Bruised for Our Iniquities

Hardly anyone remembers this way that Jesus bled, and usually it's the last place where people apply the blood. This section is mentioned last because it presents the greatest problem in most Christians' lives.

The Bible is very clear that Jesus was bruised.

> *But he was wounded for our transgressions,* **he was bruised for our iniquities**: *the chastisement of our peace was upon him; and with his stripes we are healed.*
>
> *Isaiah 53:5*

A bruise is an internal injury. Often times we do not even know where a bruise came from, but all of a sudden we see it. The way that Jesus bled to redeem us from our inward iniquities is quite revealing.

> *And some began to spit on him, and to cover his face, and to buffet him, and to say unto him, Prophesy: and the servants did strike him with the palms of their hands.*
>
> *Mark 14:65*

As the temple guards beat Jesus with their fists and open palms, they bruised the Lord all over His face. It is also reasonable to consider that they kicked Him and beat Him all over His body. Blood vessels ruptured beneath the surface of His skin and His blood was shed, but not visibly. He bled internally. It hurt just as much, and possibly even more, but there was little outward sign of injury.

This is how iniquity works. It lives on the inside. No one sees it and only the person carrying it knows its pain.

Notice that Mark 14:65 states they covered His face. This gesture is also relevant to understanding iniquity. We do not see where the iniquity comes from because it is usually generational and we often do not know the exact source.

> *Our fathers have sinned, and are not; and we have borne their iniquities.*
>
> *Lamentations 5:7*

We are going to study the subject of iniquity in great detail within the next section. We will see the generational origin and the reason why God charges it to a person's lineage. Suffice it to say, at this point, that iniquity could come from any of your ancestors to at least the third or fourth generations. That represents about thirty people (or more) that could have contributed to the iniquity in your life. This is why it says the Lord was hit and bruised with His face covered. You do not see it coming, nor where it came from, but you can most certainly feel the pain.

The Bible says that Jesus was bruised for our iniquities.

> *But he was wounded for our transgressions, **he was bruised for our iniquities**: the chastisement of our peace was upon him; and with his stripes we are healed.*
>
> *Isaiah 53:5*

These inward generational torments plague us our whole lives—until we realize Jesus' blood was shed for them to be removed.

> *Who gave himself for us, **that he might redeem us from all iniquity**, and purify unto himself a peculiar people, zealous of good works.*
>
> *Titus 2:14*

This verse declares He purified unto himself a zealous people. This means that when people who are tormented with iniquity are freed, they could very well become the greatest zealots. The curse is reversed and will yield a greater blessing of deliverance when the inward pain is gone. When someone has been tormented by a lust problem and is delivered from it, this person will probably become a great advocate in helping others to overcome related problems.

Iniquity is an inward problem and because it is generational, people often accept that "this is just the way I am." That is true until they realize that Jesus bled a particular way for this inward problem to be abolished.

In my study of iniquity, I have discovered that perhaps this is the most ignored issue regarding redemption. Because of this ignorance, people are living under bondage that was paid for at Calvary. Even though deliverance legally became theirs the day they were saved, the inward problems of anger, lust, fear, and pride are destroying people and families around the world. If only the word could reach them—Jesus was bruised for our iniquities.

The salient truth about iniquity is that there are certain transgressions worthy of death that our ancestors have committed. Because God has foreknowledge and knows that He will have children born of that lineage at a future time, He spreads the payment to the third and fourth generations, instead of killing the guilty perpetrator. The most predominate iniquities spreading over mankind are fear, lust, anger, and pride.

When we apply the blood of Jesus which He shed when He was bruised for our iniquities, the cause of continually sinning and transgressing against the commandments of God will be abolished because the iniquity is purged. Instead of being perpetually tormented by inward urges, we can face temptations with an inner strength and resolve. It is still necessary to come apart from the accused thing and depart from it, but now we have the strength to overcome by the blood of Jesus.

> *Nevertheless the foundation of God standeth sure, having this seal, The Lord knoweth them that are his. And, Let every one that nameth the name of Christ depart from iniquity.*
>
> *2 Timothy 2:19*

God is at work within us, and we can do all things through Christ who strengthens us from the inside. Instead of being bruised and hurt on the inside, we can be free of pain and guilt by the blood of Jesus.

While teaching this subject in Michigan (just before we applied the blood of Jesus through confession), a dear sister once asked me a question. "Do you mean that if I confess the iniquity of fear in my life, due to my ancestral transgressions, that I can be free from depression?" I assured her that she could and would, based on the good name of God and faith in the blood of Jesus Christ. She applied His blood and is now free! I tell you as I told her, "This is easy, because Calvary was tough." You may think this is free, and to you it may be, but Jesus paid for it with blood—His blood. He was bruised for our iniquities.

In summary, it would be a good idea to re-read this section after the following section has been covered. This is because when we realize where the blood should be applied (sin, iniquity, and transgression) then the understanding of each of the ways Jesus bled will become more meaningful. Perhaps mental weakness is a one-time problem of doubting or maybe it is a generational problem. Maybe you once made a wrong decision that the blood shed out of Jesus' feet will cover, or perhaps it is a perpetual problem that indicates iniquity.

Rest assured, whether you are dealing with a sin, iniquity, or transgression, Jesus bled for you—not only to be forgiven, but to be healed and strengthened. Each of the ways He bled has a unique significance and the Holy Spirit will reveal to you the area where you need to focus.

The following chart will summarize the ways that Jesus bled, what it forgives, and the corresponding strengthening that is a result. It will prepare us to engage the ministry of Jesus Christ, our High Priest, and to apply the wonderful, everlasting, atoning blood of Jesus.

Ways that Jesus Bled:	Sins, Transgressions or Iniquities Forgiven:	Resulting Blessing (When the Curse is Turned into a Blessing):
Out of His hands	To forgive all the deeds done by our hands	To purge our hands and make them instruments of righteousness
Out of His feet	To forgive us of the wrong decisions we have made	To endue us with wisdom to walk and be led by the Holy Spirit
Out of His back	To forgive the sins we have committed against our bodies	To give us health and strength to face corrupting flesh and the inevitability of physical death
Out of His crown	To forgive us of the sins, transgressions or iniquities of idolatry	To reign in life by Jesus Christ and to strengthen our commitment to our first love
Out of His side	To forgive our transgressions	To strengthen our heart commitment in order to make deliberate decisions for Him
Out of His brow	To forgive our mental weaknesses of fear, doubt, anxiety or worry	To give us inward strength to not vacillate on issues of the heart
He was bruised	To forgive our iniquities of fear, lust, anger and pride	To strengthen us in our inward character and to change the way we were born ("shapen in iniquity," according to Psalm 51:5)

Perfect Redemption

As we now proceed to study where and how to apply these ways that Jesus bled, we will move toward the reality we are pursuing— perfect redemption.

PART THREE

Where to Apply the Blood

Now that the seven ways that Jesus bled have been discussed, we can begin to explore our application of the blood. The blood that was shed in the Old Testament had to be applied and the blood shed in the New Covenant needs to be applied, too.

Jesus revealed in Luke 22:20 that the cup he offered was the blood of the New Covenant which was shed for them. But didn't the apostles need to take the cup and drink it? Likewise, we should drink the cup of the New Covenant and learn to apply the blood of Jesus.

We can learn *how* to apply the blood and *where* to apply the blood of Jesus by looking at Old Covenant profiles. In the Old Covenant the High Priest applied the blood on the Day of Atonement by sprinkling the blood seven times before the mercy seat. On Passover, each family took the blood of the lamb and applied it to the door of the house in three places. The seven sprinklings illustrate that the blood needs to be applied in the various ways we have discussed in the last chapter. Now the profile of the three places on the door shows us where to apply the blood. These are to our sins, iniquities, and transgressions.

PERFECT REDEMPTION

One of the greatest misconceptions and mistranslations in the entire Bible deals with the word "sin." We have been taught by word and song that the blood of Jesus is applied to our sin, but when we see the truth of what the word "sin" means, we will find exactly where the blood of Jesus needs to be applied.

Yes, the blood of Jesus is applied to our sins, but this is not the whole truth, only one-third of it. His blood atones for three kinds of wrongs: sin, transgression, and iniquity. Not knowing about transgressions and iniquities, and how to apply the blood of Jesus to them, is perhaps the most direct cause of defeat in a Christian's life. When we apply His blood only to sin, we are not receiving the full benefits of the atonement. When we apply His blood to all three, however, we receive the full deliverance Jesus paid for.

In Part Three, we will explore the true meaning of the word "sin" and thereby discover exactly where to apply the blood of the New Covenant. We will examine iniquity, the most deadly aspect of the three wrongs, and how to eradicate it from our lives. This portion of our study is absolutely vital. Even after we have seen the seven ways the blood was shed, we now need to see where the blood of Jesus must be applied if we are going to receive perfect redemption.

Chapter 6

Three Wrongs Atoned:
Sin, Transgression, and Iniquity

When God in His Word wants to communicate the complete aspect of any subject, He does this by presenting that aspect in a group of three. We can see this in many illustrations: the three persons of the Godhead are the Father, Son, and Holy Spirit; the three parts of man are spirit, soul, and body; the three parts of the tabernacle are the outer court, holy place, and Holy of Holies; and the three profits of the Word of God are doctrine, reproof, and correction. The reason the blood of Jesus was shed is for forgiveness of all our wrongs. These also are set in a complete package of three: sins, transgressions, and iniquities.

In most Christian circles, only sins are mentioned in regard to the cleansing power of Jesus' blood. The blood of Jesus does forgive our sins and we are thankful to hear it mentioned in preaching messages and in the songs we sing; but additional understanding about transgressions and iniquities will give us more information about our redemption and deliverance. The reason we only hear about sin is because we have missed a foundational transition from the Hebrew, Old Testament language to the Greek, New Testament language.

Perfect Redemption

The word "sin" in the Greek text of the New Testament is the word *hamartia*. This New Testament term includes all of the Old Testament terms regarding sin, iniquity, and transgression, but because it was translated as *sin*, we have missed the other two errors that the blood covers. This word simply means to miss the mark, as an archer would when trying to hit a bull's eye on a target. Why an archer would miss the target is explained by the Hebrew words for sin, transgression, and iniquity.

The reasons why a target is missed describe the Hebrew concepts of sin, transgression, or iniquity. An archer may miss his mark unintentionally or even intentionally, or perhaps he may have a flaw in his shooting method. Likewise, there are three different ways we may miss the mark in showing ourselves approved before God.

If the Greek word *hamartia* had been translated "error" instead of *sin*, we would have far greater accuracy in our understanding. By calling it sin, we have missed transgression and iniquity, thinking it is all covered under "sin." No! The blood of Jesus covers all our errors or wrongs, of which there are three kinds—sins, transgressions, and iniquities. People who say, "The blood of Jesus covered all my sins so I don't need to deal with transgressions or iniquities," are ignorantly digging an early grave. All three errors are covered by the blood of Jesus, but the blood must be applied to all three.

Look at the New Testament usage of these concepts.

> *And you, being dead in your **sins** and the uncircumcision of your flesh, hath he quickened together with him, having forgiven you all **trespasses;** Blotting out **the handwriting of ordinances that was against us, which was contrary to us**, and took it out of the way, nailing it to his cross;*   Colossians 2:13–14

In these verses, sins are called sins, transgressions are called trespasses, and iniquities are the handwriting of ordinances which were against us and contrary to us. Call them what you want, the blood of Jesus cleanses them. But ignoring them—either due to ignorance or intentionally—keeps us from receiving all that Jesus paid for. Iniquity is often manifested in stubbornness or refusal to accept that there may be things you do not know. This will surely keep any or all of us out of the flow of God's divine blessing.

In the next section of this chapter, the definitions of these words and their interrelationship will be examined. Before studying them individually, let's look at the following verses where these three words and concepts are used together. According to God's Word, these words have different meanings and must be dealt with specifically when applying the blood of Jesus.

> *Keeping mercy for thousands, forgiving **iniquity** and **transgression** and **sin**, and that will by no means clear the guilty; visiting the iniquity of the fathers upon the children, and upon the children's children, unto the third and to the fourth generation.*
>
> *Exodus 34:7*

> *And Aaron shall lay both his hands upon the head of the live goat, and confess over him all the **iniquities** of the children of Israel, and all their **transgressions** in all their **sins**, putting them upon the head of the goat, and shall send him away by the hand of a fit man into the wilderness:*
>
> *Leviticus 16:21*

> *I acknowledged my **sin** unto thee, and mine **iniquity** have I not hid. I said, I will confess my **transgressions** unto the LORD; and thou forgavest the **iniquity** of my sin. Selah.*
>
> *Psalms 32:5*

> *For our **transgressions** are multiplied before thee, and our **sins** testify against us: for our **transgressions** are with us; and as for our **iniquities**, we know them.*
>
> *Isaiah 59:12*

PERFECT REDEMPTION

> *Seventy weeks are determined upon thy people and upon thy holy city, to finish the **transgression**, and to make an end of **sins**, and to make reconciliation for **iniquity**, and to bring in everlasting righteousness, and to seal up the vision and prophecy, and to anoint the most Holy.*
>
> Daniel 9:24

Sin, iniquity, and transgression are three different words, with three different meanings. They are three chargeable offenses that the blood covers, but each one must have the blood applied. Not knowing the differences between these three will not exonerate the guilty party, nor will God change the rules to accommodate our ignorance.

I was in India some years ago and I went for a morning run on the beach. While on my way, I passed by an Indian man on a bicycle. He had an old straw hat on his head, a torn, dirty shirt, and ragged pants. He had a cigarette hanging out of his mouth (which had very dirty teeth in it), but the most blatant characteristic about him was the dark, lightless, hopeless glare in his eyes.

Just then the Lord spoke to me and said, "Do you know the difference between him and you?" "No sir," I responded. The Lord then said, "You know the truth that has set you free." This left a deep mark in my soul, knowing that God does not love any of us any more than any other. Some of us have heard more of the truth than others.

The truths of sin, iniquity, and transgression are specifically relevant to being set free. Oh how I wish I could have stopped the Indian man that morning and told him about iniquity and the blood of Jesus. It did not happen that day but maybe someday, somehow, a minister carrying the word of reconciliation will find him.

We have seen these words, sin, iniquity, and transgression in the Old Testament, but these truths are widened in the New Testament. The word for "transgression" in the Old Testament is the same concept and word as "trespass" in the New Testament.

> *And you hath he quickened, who were dead in*
> ***trespasses** and **sins**;*
>
> *Ephesians 2:1*

> *Saying, Blessed are they whose **iniquities** are for-*
> *given, and whose **sins** are covered.*
>
> *Romans 4:7*

Look at the New Testament application of the Old Testament usage in Hebrews 8:12 and 13.

> *For I will be merciful to their unrighteousness, and*
> *their **sins** and their **iniquities** will I remember no*
> *more. In that he saith, A new covenant, he hath*
> *made the first old. Now that which decayeth and*
> *waxeth old is ready to vanish away.*
>
> *Hebrews 8:12–13*

These words—sins, transgressions, and iniquities—are all included within the Greek word *hamartia*. If we think of these as the three kinds of error that the blood cleanses, we will have the proper understanding. The blood has been shed, now we are learning where to apply the blood.

Paint the Three Surfaces of the Door

God communicated the truth of three wrongs at the first Passover when He had three surfaces of the door painted with the blood of the lamb.

> *And they shall take of the blood, and strike it on the*
> ***two side posts** and on the **upper door post** of the*
> *houses, wherein they shall eat it.*
>
> *Exodus 12:7*

When the blood was applied to the door on the night of the Passover, you can be sure no one said, "One or maybe two places should be enough." This was probably the only time in history when a man was thankful for his wife telling him he missed a place when painting. Each surface had to be covered or they would not be "passed over."

The covering of protection behind a door shows up in other places in the Word of God. (We will find in chapter 10 that we are now behind the door of Jesus Christ's protection since He is our High Priest and door of the sheepfold.) Behind a door, according to biblical interpretation, often means protection—like when the angels were in Lot's house in Sodom and Gomorrah (Genesis 19:5–6), or when the apostles were behind closed doors for fear of the Jews.

The first usage of a door in the entire Bible indicates protection from sin when God said to Cain, "If you do well, will you not be accepted? And if you do not do well, sin lies at the **door**" (Genesis 4:7a NKJ). Sin lies at the door of our lives and the only protection we have is the blood of Jesus. (The problem with Cain's offering was that it had no blood.) The second usage of door is the door of the ark that Noah made (Genesis 6:16–18). Behind it also was protection from God's wrath.

Jesus also spoke of God's protection behind a door in Matthew 12:43–45.

> *When the unclean spirit is gone out of a man, he walketh through dry places, seeking rest, and findeth none. Then he saith, I will return into my house from whence I came out; and when he is come, he findeth it empty, swept, and garnished. Then goeth he, and taketh with himself seven other spirits more wicked than himself, and they enter in [the unprotected door] and dwell there: and the last state of that man is worse than the first. Even so shall it be also unto this wicked generation.*
> *Matthew 12:43–45*

This is a forecastable outcome concerning what happens to people when they only paint one surface of the door—meaning they deal only with sin and, even in ignorance, do not deal with iniquity or transgression. Think of the numbers of Christians who are prime targets for demonic attack because they do not know about applying the blood of Jesus to transgressions or iniquities. It's enough to make us shudder.

Sin, transgression, and iniquity completes the package of wrongs that the blood of Jesus atones. There is hardly a more applicable lesson in all of Christianity. As we learn about each one of these errors, we will be able to understand how to deal with them by learning how to apply—and *where* to apply—the blood of Jesus to each of them.

The Basic Definitions

The basic definitions for sin, transgression, and iniquity illustrate that they are different words with different concepts, and there is a need to have the blood of Jesus applied to each of them. The definitions given below are simple and have a simple application. There is certainly more specific information to know about these words, and the more we know about them, the more equipped we will be to teach about them and receive blessings.[14]

◆ **Sin** is an unintentional wrong. It is an action committed in ignorance, without knowledge. It is an error done in ignorance.

◆ **Transgression** is a wrong committed with full knowledge. It means to know better but to do it anyway. It is an error done with full knowledge.

◆ **Iniquity** is an inner perverseness which prompts a person to repetitively commit either a sin or a transgression. Instead of an action committed, it is the motive that compels the carrier to commit the offense.

Looking at Exodus 34:7, we can see that these are distinctly different words. Sin is the Hebrew word *chattaah*, transgression is *pesha*, and iniquity is *avon*.

> *"Keeping mercy for thousands, forgiving **iniquity** **[avon]** and **transgression [pesha]** and **sin [chattaah]**, and that will by no means clear the guilty; visiting the iniquity of the fathers upon the children, and upon the children's children, unto the third and to the fourth generation."*
>
> *Exodus 34:7*

These are three different words and concepts, but as different as they are, they have close relationships with one another. When searching the whole scope of the Bible for these words, we find that they are used over 500 times in related verses and scriptural context. As we have discussed before, these three make a complete package. This is a big deal.

Beyond a doubt, the most intricate of these wrongs and the one that requires more study to understand is iniquity. From its definition, we observe that it is the motive or cause of continual sins or transgressions. When you eradicate this motive, then the nagging torment and cause for repetitive errors will vanish. Ezekiel 21:24 demonstrates this.

> *Therefore thus saith the Lord GOD; Because ye have made your **iniquity** to be remembered, in that your **transgressions** are discovered, so that in all your doings your **sins** do appear; because, I say, that ye are come to remembrance, ye shall be taken with the hand.*
>
> *Ezekiel 21:24*

Whenever transgressions or sins appear or reappear, it is because iniquities are remembered. This is the relationship between these entities. An iniquity is the root cause for repetitive sins and transgressions to be committed. When the iniquity is removed the compelling cause behind continual sin or transgression is gone. Yes, deliverance *is* available.

Why is it that people show up at the altar to confess the same error time and time again? Is it because they are just weak willed and fall prey to temptation, or is there a greater reality working behind the scenes?

I have a good friend and spiritual brother, Larry Hutto, who is the pastor of Living Waters Fellowship in Barnwell, South Carolina. While I was teaching the class *Perfect Redemption*, he learned about iniquity and how to apply the blood of Jesus to it. His own deliverance was so powerful that he wrote this testimony:

> "During a *Perfect Redemption* teaching session with Dale Sides, the truth of the iniquity of my fathers and its effects on my life was revealed. The Holy Spirit revealed that I was under the effect of anxiety and that it was a generational problem.
>
> Since childhood I had had an insatiable need to learn and understand. It would frequently become annoying and obsessive. I struggled mentally to search and find reasons for everything from the trivial to the profound. The result of this constant mental activity was minimal sleep, frustration, and intense mental and emotional pressure.
>
> As I embraced this truth [about iniquity] and followed the biblical instructions during the class, God brought super-natural release in many areas of my life, especially in my head. At that precise moment [when I confessed my iniquities], I felt as if a valve had been opened in my head, releasing all this pressure.
>
> Today, I marvel and rejoice in this release of anxiety and the receiving of such perfect peace, simplicity of life, and confidence in my relationship with God, my family, and the ministry."

This is the statement of a wonderful man, committed to serving the Lord for more than twenty-five years. However, he had a tormenting iniquity that caused him anxiety and mental discomfort. He did not know that it was paid for almost 2,000 years ago. Worry and anxiety were the sins (Philippians 4:6 NKJ, Romans 14:23b) that represented the baggage and dead weight (Hebrews 12:1) that Pastor Hutto had to deal with continually. He discovered what we are about to see. **The blood of Jesus was shed to remove our iniquities, and once the blood has been applied to the iniquity, the sins and transgressions that it causes will cease to torment us.**

The New Testament clearly affirms that there is a relationship between sins and transgressions (trespasses) as they relate to iniquity. It declares that blotting out the ordinances against us (our iniquity) is how we are made alive and that sins and transgressions are forgiven.

> *And you, being dead in your **sins** and the uncircumcision of your flesh, hath he quickened together with him, having forgiven you all **trespasses**; Blotting out **the handwriting of ordinances that was against us, which was contrary to us**, and took it out of the way, nailing it to his cross;*
>
> *Colossians 2:13–14*

Hebrews 10:17 shows these words used together and the direct correlation between sin and iniquity.

> *And their **sins** and **iniquities** will I remember no more.*
>
> *Hebrews 10:17*

Iniquity and its effect is the root cause of generational curses and repetitive torment in people's lives. Jesus' blood has been shed for these torments to be removed. The sad news is that because people are ignorant about applying His blood, they are still walking around in bondage.

The clarion truth about generational curses is rooted in an understanding of iniquity. This is of such dire importance that we need to invest our time to study and learn about this subject. In so doing, we will gain vital understanding about this missing piece of the puzzle regarding deliverance and where to apply the blood of Jesus.

But he was wounded for our transgressions, he was bruised for our iniquities: the chastisement of our peace was upon him; and with his stripes we are healed.

Isaiah 53:5

Chapter 7

Understanding Iniquity

S ins and transgressions are actions people take, but iniquity is the inner force that prompts the carrier to commit the wrongs. The fact that there were both sin and trespass offerings in the Old Testament but no offering for iniquity further bears this out. As previously mentioned, iniquity is biblically defined as an inner, invisible force that compels an individual to commit sins and transgressions. The fact that it is an *inner* force emphasizes a most crucial point in the book of Isaiah. Isaiah prophesies of Jesus Christ in chapter 53 verse 5 that He was bruised for our iniquities.

> *But he was wounded for our transgressions, **he was bruised for our iniquities:** the chastisement of our peace was upon him; and with his stripes we are healed.*
>
> *Isaiah 53:5*

A bruise is an inward injury, often unnoticed by others, but it causes the bearer severe pain. We call inward injuries bruises when they appear on the surface, but deep down inside they are hemorrhages. Both bruises and hemorrhages are potentially the most dangerous kind of injury because they are not seen, and if left untreated can cause death with little or no forewarning. Both cause agonizing pain that cannot be seen by any other person. Internal injury is the particular characteristic of an iniquity. A bruise is internal, further indicating that an iniquity is an internal matter, also. Jesus also referred to iniquity as an inward reality.

> *Even so ye also outwardly appear righteous unto men, but* **within ye are full of** *hypocrisy and* **iniquity***.*
>
> *Matthew 23:28*

In verse 27 of Matthew 23, Jesus also compared the Pharisees with whited sepulchres—they looked good on the outside, but within they were full of iniquity. This is the way iniquity works. It is an inward torment or pain that goes unnoticed by others. These internal injuries can cause someone to drop dead spiritually and no one else has any idea that anything is wrong. The deepest and longest lasting pain of any of the wrongs that Jesus bled for is iniquity— the root cause of most people's problems.

In this chapter, we are going to discover the cause of iniquity and see that it is the generational root cause of a person's greatest dysfunction. When it is generational, people are born with it and that makes it very hard to recognize that anything is out of the ordinary. The person will accept that "this is just the way I am." The primary reason for devoting this whole chapter to understanding iniquity is so we can recognize it and then apply the blood of Jesus to it.

Before proceeding any further in our discussion, we need to remember that iniquity has been put under the blood of Jesus and can be removed just as sin or transgression can be removed. The fact that iniquity is rarely identified may make it seem like an insurmountable problem, but every problem seems that way until the proper solution is applied. Do not despair over iniquity! The blood of Jesus was shed for it to be forgiven and to remove it from the place of infamy it now occupies.

We are also going to discover that this inward pain (iniquity) is the nagging torment that causes people to repeat the same sins or transgressions continually. This will explain many things. For example, why do people (despite the desire to be delivered) have recurring problems and show up at the altar for confession again and again? Some of these people have deep discipline in their lives in all other areas, but one particular area always seems to elude deliverance. Likewise, why does an age-old saint of God who has been a faithful Christian for many, many years suddenly walk away from the faith? The answer usually is that they have been nursing a hidden iniquitous bruise that finally brings a disastrous end to a beautiful person.

Not too long ago I was conducting a class on *Perfect Redemption* with a group of over five hundred ministers. When I asked them if they knew what iniquity was only three out of five hundred knew what it was. As scary as that was, only one of them knew how to deal with it. These were the ministers. Hello, Houston—we have a problem!

This is truly one of the most obscured truths in the whole Bible. When iniquity is finally understood, it will seem almost as if a miracle cure has been given to a dying patient. For this reason, we need to invest our time and energy and learn about this devastation and how to apply the blood of Jesus to this tormenting spiritual plague, otherwise the redemption would not be complete.

The First Usage of Iniquity

To properly learn about iniquity, we need to apply a biblical research key known as the law of first usage. This law simply means that more credence must be given to the first time a word is used in the Bible than at other times. In short, the Bible defines its own terms. (It does predate Noah Webster.)

"Iniquity" and its related concept appear quite early in the Bible; it is attributed to Cain. After Cain had murdered his brother Abel and God exacted punishment upon him, Cain's reply contains the very first usage of the word we call iniquity. It is the Hebrew word *avon* and we find it first in Genesis 4:13, where it has been translated as "punishment."

> *And Cain said unto the LORD, My punishment [avon] is greater than I can bear.*
>
> *Genesis 4:13*

Avon has 231 usages in the Old Testament. 215 usages are translated "iniquity" and the other 16 are rendered "punishment" in some form. Both translations of iniquity and punishment have valid contributions to the understanding of the Hebrew word. Iniquity shows that it is an inward twist or perversion; punishment illustrates that it has a long-lasting effect.

The accepted definition of *avon* is "a perversity," according to the Strong's #5771. The root meaning, from *avah*, means "a twist" or "to be crooked." When we combine this information with the fact that iniquity is an inward problem, we derive the understanding of "an inward force that causes a person to be twisted in some way." When we add the "punishment" perspective, we also see the long-lasting, even generational, aspect.

In most English dictionaries, the synonym "wicked" is offered in the definition of iniquity. The same concept is communicated as the Hebrew word *avah* because the root word of wicked "wicca" (an Old English word) also means twisted. A wick is a twisted cord. Likewise, wicker furniture is made from twisted fibers from a particular plant. So, "wicked" really is a synonym for iniquity; however, its derivation is not just as an evil or cruel thing, but is caused by something being intrinsically twisted in form. This shows that iniquity is the underlying cause for someone to be evil or cruel.

The Greek word for iniquity in the New Testament is the word *anomos*. Its root meaning is "lawlessness." This definition offers an additional insight to the inward twisting. It causes the bearer to think, "I am the *exception* and the rules do not apply to me." This is particularly manifested in Cain because he refused to offer sacrifice properly, even after being offered a second chance by God.

The aspect of having an "inward twist" is directly depicted in Cain. The twist in Cain that caused him to murder his brother was evident in his life before he actually killed Abel. It is revealed earlier in Genesis 4:5 when Cain manifested anger with God. It was the iniquity of anger that eventually manifested itself in the transgression of murder.

> But He [God] did not respect Cain and his offering.
> And Cain was very **angry**, and his countenance fell.
> *Genesis 4:5 NKJ*

Cain was twisted with anger. It was an inner force that drove him. The Bible relates that he first got angry with God and then Abel. In reality he was probably angry with Adam and quickly following, angry with himself. Then he got to God and ultimately Abel. Regardless of the order, he had a propensity towards anger.

Iniquity is the inner force that causes someone to sin or transgress. This means that iniquity is the root cause, and sin or transgression is the result. To say this another way: iniquity is the motive and sin or transgression is the resulting action. For Cain, the iniquity of anger was manifested in the sin of murder.

What a fantastic revelation! Now that we have discovered that iniquity is the cause of repetitive sins and transgressions, and since we know that the blood of Jesus can remove iniquity, we are beginning to realize that nagging recurring problems and their torment can be abolished as well.

Jesus openly discussed the relationship between inward unresolved iniquity and the outward manifestations of sins and transgressions in Matthew 5. He said that the root problem with murder is really anger, and the inward cause of adultery is really lust.

> *Ye have heard that it was said of them of old time,*
> *Thou shalt not **kill**; and whosoever shall kill shall be*
> *in danger of the judgment: But I say unto you, That*
> *whosoever is **angry** with his brother without a cause*
> *shall be in danger of the judgment.*
>
> Matthew 5:21,22a

> *But I say unto you, That whosoever looketh on a*
> *woman to **lust** after her hath committed **adultery***
> *with her already in his heart.*
>
> Matthew 5:28

We have seen from the Old Testament definition and also from the New Testament teachings of Jesus (both from the issue of iniquity in the Pharisees and the relationships between anger and murder and lust and adultery), that iniquity is an inward perverseness. These verses document that iniquity is the real hidden issue behind sins and transgressions.

Not only did Jesus openly teach that iniquity is the inward cause of sins and transgressions such as adultery or murder, but Paul testified of the cleansing power of redemption in overcoming iniquity.

> *Who gave himself for us, **that he might redeem us***
> ***from all iniquity**, and purify unto himself a peculiar*
> *people, zealous of good works.*
>
> Titus 2:14

There is hope on the horizon for those of us who have been tormented and plagued with recurring problems. Inward pains such as anger, lust, fear or pride are not insurmountable problems. Parents with children manifesting the same sins and transgressions as they have now know why their children are commiting them. There is light at the end of the tunnel and hope for those who have been hopeless. As we press further into this topic, we will discover that the inward bruises of iniquities in us, as well as in our children, can be forgiven and healed by the blood of Jesus.

Understanding Iniquity

The Cause of Iniquity

We discussed the first usage of iniquity in the canon of the Word of God, but the first time it happened chronologically was not with Cain but with Lucifer.

> *Thou [Lucifer] wast perfect in thy ways from the day that thou wast created, till **iniquity** was found in thee.*
>
> *Ezekiel 28:15*

According to the context of Ezekiel 28, the inner force that compelled Lucifer to commit sin was greed and rebellion. Since God created him with a free will, he had the freedom to choose good or evil. He began to desire the things that belonged to God, and according to Isaiah 14:12ff, he merchandized the worship of angels. His own inner cravings and desire corrupted his perfection. Verse 16 states specifically that inner rage manifested itself in sin and that the cause of sin was the inward iniquity.

> *By the multitude of thy merchandise they have filled the midst of thee with violence, and **thou hast sinned**:*
>
> *Ezekiel 28:16a*

So Lucifer, therefore, is the father of iniquity. By a calculated guess, this is what he transferred to the angels who were deposed with him also. He proceeded to corrupt Adam and Eve and their inner purity. Once the iniquity was started, it spread throughout mankind because it is generationally transmitted. This will finally culminate in the antichrist who will be so generationally bent and inwardly twisted that the "mystery of iniquity" will produce a man who says that he is God (2 Thessalonians 2:3–7).

The Generational Cause of Iniquity

Iniquity can come from someone not controlling their mind and yielding to evil by their own will, such as Lucifer, but the predominant usage of iniquity stems from a cause and root within mankind that is passed down generational lines. An explanation is necessary, since it seems unfair that God would charge an offense to a person when someone else committed the act. When we understand why He did this, we will once again see God's mercy at work.

One of the hottest topics in Christianity now is generational curses. Generational curses are really nothing more than iniquity with a modern title. Understanding iniquity will explain the reasoning behind generational curses and why God charges them to a subsequent generation. In the process, it will help to explain the most difficult person you have ever had to deal with—you. At the same time, this will generate a new compassion for others, including your mother-in-law and boss, when you realize what has been "pushing their buttons."

Look at these usages from the Bible that connect generational relationships to iniquity.

> *Our fathers have sinned, and are not; and we have borne their iniquities.*
>
> *Lamentations 5:7*

> *We have sinned with our fathers, we have committed iniquity, we have done wickedly.*
>
> *Psalm 106:6*

> *Let the iniquity of his fathers be remembered with the LORD; and let not the sin of his mother be blotted out.*
>
> *Psalms 109:14*

> *God layeth up his iniquity for his children: he rewardeth him, and he shall know it.*
>
> *Job 21:19*

This next usage is the first place in the Bible where sin, transgression, and iniquity are used together. It also demonstrates that there is individual iniquity as well as generational iniquity.

> *"Keeping mercy for thousands, forgiving **iniquity** and **transgression** and **sin**, by no means clearing the guilty; visiting **the iniquity of the fathers** upon the children and the children's children to the third and the fourth generation."*
>
> *Exodus 34:7*

The reason why God charges iniquity to a generation is fascinating. It demonstrates God's mercy. This explanation reverts back to the first bearer of iniquity and his father, Cain and Adam.

Why God Charges Iniquity

As we begin to study why God charges iniquity, we will see a brand new manifestation of mercy. I have mentioned before that iniquity is the root cause of generational curses. If God did not charge it He would have to kill the perpetrator and thereby destroy the lineage and potential children from that lineage.

People have said, "It is unfair for God to charge me for something I did not do." A man once said to me, "I had absolutely nothing to do with what my father did. Why should I pay for it?" Similarly, that man had absolutely nothing to do with being born. By the same token, if he shouldn't have to pay for generational iniquities, then shouldn't he have to pay for being born? Honoring your father and mother is the first commandment with promise. It is not a wise thing to "jump the gun" and unjustly charge God and tell Him how to run the universe. Remember that Cain got angry with God and anytime you see someone doing this it is still iniquity at work.

We will see that God, in His mercy, has allowed us to live and that He does not charge the *sins* of a generation, but the iniquities. (This is another benefit of understanding the differences between sins, iniquities, and transgressions.) Also, remember that God has made a way for these to be forgiven.

Let us go back to the beginning before mankind had sin, transgression, or iniquity. God said to Adam that the day that Adam ate of the tree of the knowledge of good and evil he would die. We have assumed that because Adam did not physically expire, "death" meant that he spiritually died, or lost the indwelling presence of the Holy Spirit. This may very well be true, but there is also another explanation.

Hebrews 6:18 says that it is impossible for God to lie, and since He had promised the sentence of death to Adam, He had to demand payment for the wrong. God knew that all of this would transpire, so He had a "Plan B" waiting in the wings.

What we must realize is that God is omniscient and He knew that if He "snuffed" Adam there would not be any offspring and the whole race of mankind would be annihilated. Yes, the offender would have gotten exactly what he deserved, but then none of his children would ever have been born. In order to maintain His integrity and not lie, God initiated Plan B. (Not only can God not lie, He also cannot be surprised.) He spread the death penalty due to Adam over the coming generations. As opposed to this punishment that would have preempted their lives, God chose, by His mercy, to let them live but to shoulder the burden of the ancestral transgression.

Verses 18 and 19 of the seventh chapter of Micah illustrate this truth.

> *Who is a God like unto thee, that pardoneth **iniquity**, and passeth by the **transgression** of the remnant of his heritage? he retaineth not his anger for ever, because he delighteth in mercy. He will turn again, he will have compassion upon us; he will subdue our **iniquities**; and thou wilt cast all their **sins** into the depths of the sea.*   *Micah 7:18–19*

God delights in mercy. If He did not, He would have killed Adam on the spot. God's mercy was to pardon the transgression, but charge the iniquity, so all His (and Adam's) children could be born at a later time. If He killed the transgressor, the transgressor would not bear any children or children's children's children.

In fact, iniquity is a commuted death sentence prorated over three or four generations. It is charged to the offender and then passed down through the lineage. It will show up as a tendency, a propensity, or a "bent" in the victim. It is important to note, however, that if the bearer, or progeny, of the offender commits a similar sin or transgression, the condition is renewed and in fact, the iniquity becomes even stronger than before. This is how races of people and even nationalities become known for their particular "less than admirable traits," i.e., Irish and alcohol, Italians and anger, and Latinos and lust.

It is my belief that iniquity is passed down to the offspring by the spirit of man at the time of conception. The life within the zygote is called the spirit of man because it is the male that contributes the "spark" of life in the union of the sperm and the egg. Look at what Genesis 5 says about Seth.

> *And Adam lived an hundred and thirty years, and begat a son in his own likeness, and after his image; and called his name Seth:*
>
> *Genesis 5:3*

When Adam and Eve conceived Cain, Abel, and Seth they were in the likeness and image of Adam. This means that the sentence of death in Adam passed to his entire lineage, and ultimately to you and me too. It is this life of the father, with all its power and potential, in combination with the chromosomal contribution of the egg from the mother, that directs the DNA development of each person and finally the genetic potential and therefore the iniquitous tendencies within each person.

There is also a good possibility that iniquitous tendencies of the spirit of man are deposited in the recessive gene codes of a person.[15] This would show why greater iniquitous tendencies exist for some people if the mother carries the same recessive genes as the father, not to mention the dominant ones. If the iniquity of the spirit is deposited and carried through a recessive gene, then both father and mother would contribute to it. This possibility could explain why Abel apparently did not share the tendency toward anger that Cain had, because the trait was recessive, not dominant, and therefore not predictable. This could also be true of the third or fourth generation, because a recessive gene may not manifest itself in the second or third generation.

To the best of my knowledge the Bible strongly refers generational curses and iniquities back to the fathers. Mothers, however, surely contribute to the gene code and therefore, if the recessive gene theory is valid, contribute some tendencies, too. It does appear that because the mother may be the greater contributor to the environment regarding how a child is raised, she would therefore influence the way a person will grow or the way the iniquity may manifest. If the iniquity of the father and the environment of the family, as directed by the mother, establishes or reinforces the iniquity propensity, it is most likely the sin or transgression will be repeated in the offspring. The particular way a child is raised will determine in what way the iniquity is manifested.

These possibilities are congruous with the logic of Scripture, but are certainly way past the point of being guaranteed. One thing is certain—that iniquity within a lineage has a tendency to get worse and worse. Cain and his ensuing lineage down to Lamech (Genesis 4:23) document this, and the nations of the world demonstrate this tendency too. (Thank God for the blood of Jesus.)

King David is an excellent example of how generational traits are passed down. Remember that if God "offed" the transgressor who was worthy of death, He would have cut off His own lineage. God made the promise to David that an heir would sit on the throne forever. God had to prorate the sentence of death to David instead of killing him since Solomon, an ancestor of the Messiah, had not yet been born when David committed two transgressions punishable by death—adultery and murder.

Remember the account: God promised David that He would give him an heir to sit on his throne (2 Samuel7:12–16) and to his kingdom there would be no end. David, however, had an adulterous affair with Bathsheba later. Then in order to hide it, he had her husband, Uriah, killed. These were two transgressions punishable by death. But if God enforced the death penalty against David, then God's word concerning the heir to the Messianic line would have been broken—since Solomon, the next in succession (2 Chronicles 28:5), had not yet been born.

It is interesting that David said, "I was shapen in iniquity and in sin my mother conceived me," (Psalm 51:5). David was under the "bastard curse" of sexual impropriety from ten generations back because Judah had an adulterous encounter with Tamar, his daughter-in-law.[16] So, when David saw Bathsheba bathing herself, the recessive iniquity traits in David went off like a rocket. Though David had to be held accountable, God knew his frame and remembered he was dust. Father Yahweh delights in mercy, and the great grandfather (to the fourteenth generation) of Jesus Christ was allowed to continue living and produce the thirteenth generation grandfather, and so on . . .

God had mercy on David and did not exact the punishment for adultery and murder on him, but these traits were passed down to David's offspring. Amnon raped his half-sister and was murdered by David's son Absalom. Absalom also went in to David's concubines in the presence of all Israel. Adonijah lost his life from lusting after David's concubine Abishag. Finally, Solomon, the heir to the throne, took the iniquity of sexual immorality and raised it into an art form with his hundreds of wives and concubines. Moreover, the love of women cost Solomon, and the nation of Israel, its prominence in the history of its time.[17] Iniquity likewise will continue to run its destructive course within the human race (2 Thessalonians 2:7).

In summary, God in His mercy and omniscience does not kill an offender that sins or transgresses by an act punishable by death. He knows if the offender will have any righteous offspring. If they will, He lets the offender live, but has to charge the death sentence to the offspring. In other words, God says, "Somebody has to pay."

We will see that Jesus stepped forward and said, "I will." Do not get lost in understanding iniquity. We are looking for understanding only to help us realize the depth of God's love and forgiveness. We will finally discover at the end of our quest that Jesus was bruised for our iniquities—and because of this we and our children can live free from generational curses. This is possible only by the grace of God and the blood of Jesus Christ.

How Generational Iniquity Is Manifested

It is important to remember that each and every person is charged only with his or her own sin or transgression, but it is iniquity that is passed down. Ezekiel 18 repeatedly states that "the soul that sins shall die," and that the sons are not charged with the sins of the fathers. The truth is that the sin is charged to the person; but when it is one worthy of death and carries a sentence of death, iniquity is charged to the generations that follow.

The law of sin and death is the "catch-all" phrase used in the New Testament regarding sins or transgressions punishable by death. (See Romans 8:2.) There were sins in the Old Testament that did not carry the death penalty. For example, if you moved a landmark, did not pen up your bull that was known to push, or touched a dead person, you were not sentenced to die. However, the major transgressions people died for included: worshipping false gods and making graven images; murder; breaking the Sabbath, or committing adultery and other related sexual sins.[18]

As previously mentioned, if a forefather committed one of these sins or transgressions, the iniquity was charged to him, but rather than killing him and preempting the existence of future children and potential worshippers, God prorated the iniquity to the following generations. The actual sin was not charged to the generations, but the iniquity was.

When iniquity is charged to a generation, a weakness will emerge if the recessive gene manifests. For example, if a man commits adultery, the lust propensity may be passed down. If a person commits murder, it is possible that anger will probably be conveyed.

By studying the scope of both the Old Testament and New Testament, comparing sections of Scripture like Romans 1:29–32 and Galatians 5:19–21, and by experience when dealing with individuals who are manifesting sins that were initiated by iniquitous tendencies, I have compiled the following chart. This chart is by no means a final word on this topic, because it is subject to my own interpretation. It will help you, however, to realize the potential background of your problem and perhaps generate some newfound compassion for others when you see there is an underlying cause behind their continual problems. It will also help you learn what you need to confess to apply the blood of Jesus where He was bruised.

You will see in this chart similar symptoms manifested by different causes. This can be due to personality types, either active or passive, or when the environment supports a specific type of sin or transgression that is committed. Please remember this chart is compiled from my interpretation of the Scriptures and my own subjective experiences.

Sins or Transgressions Punishable by Death	Iniquity Manifested in Subsequent Generations
Worshipping false gods or making graven images (includes self-worship)	**Predominantly fear.** All forms of self-consciousness, i.e., fear, worry, doubt, criticism, unforgiveness, judgment, anger, sorcery, contentiousness, witchcraft, heresy, pride . . .
Sexual impropriety, i.e., homosexuality or adultery (see Leviticus 18)	**Predominantly lust.** All forms of lust, i.e., adultery, fornication, and all forms of sexual perversions, homosexuality, bestiality, gambling, drunkenness, drug addictions, excesses of all sorts . . .
Murder	**Predominantly anger.** Envy, hatred, strife, ambition, contentiousness, criticism, judgment, gossip, bitterness, unforgiveness . . .
Dishonoring God by breaking His holy days, defaming His name, or by being indifferent to Him and rejecting your need for Him.	**Predominantly pride.** Love of money, impatience, all forms of selfishness, indifference, argumentativeness, bitterness, discrimination . . .

Removing Iniquity from Your Lineage

Hardly anything carries the weight of a threat like one of punishment to our children or our grandchildren. That is why this truth about iniquity is so impacting. We as Christians need to be raising entire lineages holy to the Lord, not forfeited to iniquity, so we must give this aspect of our lives specific attention.

We will see in the next chapter, "The Death of Iniquity," that at the time of the new birth the root of iniquity dies. But many, many people receive the Lord and the new birth after their children have been born and by then, "the die is cast." The previously mentioned manifestations of iniquity show up in children and grandchildren, so taking these remedial steps will be very important for establishing godly heritages.

Since iniquity is passed down to the third and fourth generation, it is important to learn how to deal with children and grandchildren who may be carriers. We have assumed that iniquity can be passed down through recessive genes, so if this is true, it is also difficult to determine if any, all, or none of the offspring have it.

The clarion solution to the problem is a commandment from the Lord anyway—teach and train your children! (Refer to Proverbs 22:6, Deuteronomy 11:19, and Ephesians 6:4.)

If you were carrying any unforgiven iniquity at the time of the conception of a child or children, it would be a good idea for you to sit them down and tell them about their potential or possible heritage. Tell them they are Christian born and bred. Also tell them about blessings that have been passed down to them from thousands of generations. But it is a good idea to tell them about the possibility of what they may have received from you.

It is very important for mothers to remember their input in their children's lives. They may contribute recessive genes to the iniquity package, but they especially contribute to the "rearing standards" and the established parameters of behavior. God requires that any and all bearers of iniquity live above their tendencies, so we all need to be spiritually minded and not carnally controlled. Mothers, teach your children to fear God and obey His commandments. Fathers, teach them that they may have certain tendencies in their lives and to steer clear of the pitfalls their forefathers have fallen into.

One of the most frequently asked questions I hear about children and iniquity concerns adopted children. The best answer I know is that God is a merciful God and wants all His people to have His best, but the gene pool of an adopted child does not change when the child's name does. I have seen time and time again generational tendencies flare-up in adopted children. The best solution is to teach them what they need to know about iniquity so that if or when it does show up, they will recognize it. Most especially, adopted children need to get born again and live holy lives so that the tendencies will not be passed down to their children too.

Because of the redemptive blood of Jesus, if children live holy, do not renew the condition, and apply the blood of Jesus over themselves, their children will not have a trace of the previous maladies. Remember also to teach your children to teach their children. Intergenerational teaching and training has been one of the greatest strengths in the Hebrew nation.

As we discuss "Understanding Iniquity," please remember that these offenses are redeemable and can be covered by the blood of Jesus. The previous exhortation not to despair still holds true. When these offenses are put under His blood, the root source of the continual nagging torment will be removed.

To be reminded, we are involved in a building process and are in the initial stage of learning where to apply the blood of Jesus. Sin, transgression, and iniquity are the three places where His blood must be applied. As we continue in the next chapter, "The Death of Iniquity," we will more fully appreciate the solution to this problem—the blood of Jesus.

We are focusing upon the end result of applying the blood of Jesus for perfect redemption. These truths will dovetail into spiritual understanding when the principles concerning how to apply the blood are revealed.

Who is a God like unto thee, that pardoneth iniquity, and passeth by the transgression of the remnant of his heritage? he retaineth not his anger for ever, because he delighteth in mercy. He will turn again, he will have compassion upon us; he will subdue our iniquities; and thou wilt cast all their sins into the depths of the sea.

Micah 7:18–19

Chapter 8

The Death of Iniquity

God has and always has had a plan for dealing with iniquity. When He prorated the death sentence to subsequent generations, He said, "Because I am just and cannot lie, someone has to pay." All of us carried the sentence of iniquity on us until Jesus Christ stepped forward and said, "I'll pay." Jesus paid for our iniquity to be atoned. He dealt the death blow to iniquity when the old man of sin was executed.

There is a remarkable truth contained in the Old Testament (Jeremiah 31:29–33) that prophesies of the death of iniquity. It shows that with the coming of the new covenant, iniquity dies. This truth is verified in the New Testament in the book of Hebrews (chapter 10:12–17).

The death of iniquity parallels the death of the old man in Romans 6:6 and must be applied in the same way—it must be reckoned dead. To introduce this "reckoning" we will begin with death of the old man. The old man spirit is where the roots of iniquity were born and has been since the time of conception.

The new man was made alive by the regeneration of the spirit of man when the Holy Spirit entered the spirit of man (Galatians 4:6) and recreated the spirit into life (Ephesians 2:1, 5). At the same time the new man was energized to life, the old man—the sin nature where iniquity was resident—was executed. As the life of the spirit relates to energy and electricity, the old man was "electrocuted" simultaneously as the new man was created in righteousness and true holiness. A death and a resurrection occurred within you in the twinkling of an eye.

The death of the old man sin nature marked the death of iniquity.

> *Knowing this, that our old man was crucified with Him, that the body of sin might be done away with, that we should no longer be slaves of sin.*
> *Romans 6:6 NKJ*

The body of sin refers to the spiritual body of the old man nature. Every man has a body and the old man had a spiritual body of sin. When the old man was crucified, this body was buried by baptism into death. The body of sin of the old man died when the new man was born. Along with the body and the spirit of the old man, iniquity died when the electrocution occurred.

If we do not know that the old man is dead, then we most assuredly will be in bondage to sin all the days of our lives. We *must* reckon him dead. This requires a conscious decision.

> *Likewise you also, reckon yourselves to be dead indeed to sin, but alive to God in Christ Jesus our Lord.*
> *Romans 6:11 NKJ*

The old man is your former spirit of man before the new birth. At the time of the new birth, the spirit of man is recreated in righteousness and true holiness (Ephesians 4:24) and therefore the old man, along with his nature and iniquity, dies. There is a new spirit created within the Christian. This was prophesied in the Old Testament in Ezekiel 11:19, Ezekiel 36:26, and Jeremiah 31:29–34.

> *"I will give you a new heart and put a new spirit within you; I will take the heart of stone out of your flesh and give you a heart of flesh, "I will put My*

The Death of Iniquity

> *Spirit within you and cause you to walk in My statutes, and you will keep My judgments and do them.*
>
> *Ezekiel 36:26–27 NKJ*

This new spirit is specifically shown in the book of Jeremiah (chapter 31:29–34).

> *"But this is the covenant that I will make with the house of Israel: After those days, says the LORD, I will put My law in their minds, and write it on their hearts; and I will be their God, and they shall be My people.*
>
> *Jeremiah 31:33 NKJ*

Within the same context of these verses, the death of iniquity is made evident with the coming of the new covenant. This new covenant occurs when the new spirit is created—when the old man dies and the new man is born. Verse 34 then declares, without question, the death of iniquity.

> *"No more shall every man teach his neighbor, and every man his brother, saying, 'Know the LORD,' for they all shall know Me, from the least of them to the greatest of them," says the LORD. **"For I will forgive their iniquity, and their sin I will remember no more."***
>
> *Jeremiah 31:34 NKJ*

As strong as this statement is, verses 29 and 30 emphatically assert the death of iniquity at the time of entry into the New Covenant.

> *"In those days [of the new covenant] they shall say no more: 'The fathers have eaten sour grapes, and the children's teeth are set on edge.' "But every one shall die for his own iniquity; every man who eats the sour grapes, his teeth shall be set on edge.*
>
> *Jeremiah 31:29–30 NKJ*

Viewed from the New Testament, this principle becomes so vivid that we must realize this is a major truth God wants us to recognize. Hebrews 10:15–17 emphasizes this fact.

> *Whereof the Holy Ghost also is a witness to us: for after that* **he had said before** *[from Jeremiah 31:33].*
>
> *Hebrews 10:15*

(Here is the direct quotation from Jeremiah 31:33, restated in the New Covenant—showing that these are the days of fulfillment.)

> *This is the covenant that I will make with them after those days, saith the Lord, I will put my laws into their hearts, and in their minds will I write them, And their sins and iniquities will I remember no more.*
>
> *Hebrews 10:16–17*

No more can the iniquity of the fathers be charged to the sons when the son becomes a born-again child of God. Every man shall die for his *own* iniquity.

Yes, iniquity and generational curses are very, very real for the un-regenerated person. All of us lived under them until the time of the new birth and regeneration of the new man. But when a person is born-again, the old man dies, along with the residence of the generational iniquity. Every Christian, young or old, needs to take a bold stand and tell the devil that they are dead to sin, iniquity, and transgression. These died when the old man died. Say out loud, right now, **"I am dead to iniquity."**

The problem facing Christians is that the effects of the iniquity are so impacting from the days before the new birth that it is difficult to reckon the memories dead now. These are the scenarios that are voiced as, "This is the way I am, and I always will be that way." No! The confession needs to change to: "That's the way I *was*. I am a new creation in Christ Jesus. Old things are passed away. All things are become new" (2 Corinthians 5:17).

When the Bible says "passed away" it is referred to as dead, just as when you say someone "passed away." Now you can say that the old man "passed away," and iniquity went right along with him.

This is a major truth of the new creation. We need to boldly confess: The blood of Jesus is stronger than the blood of my fathers!

We need to tell the devil that he is a liar and the father of lies. We need to confess that the old man is dead and buried and all the charges he had against us and our families went with him. Jesus took all those charges, nailed them to the cross (Colossians 2:13–14) and then took them to the grave with him. Now, we walk in newness of life (Romans 6:4).

Either the new birth is true, or we are believing a lie. It *is* true, and therefore, you are free from sin, transgression, and iniquity. They died when the old man died. Old things are passed away. All things are become new. We must continue to confess truth in the face of lies. Hebrews 10:19–23 then becomes a bulwark of confession for Christians.

> *Having therefore, brethren, boldness to enter into the holiest by the blood of Jesus, By a new and living way, which he hath consecrated for us, through the veil, that is to say, his flesh; And having an high priest over the house of God; Let us draw near with a true heart in full assurance of faith, having our hearts sprinkled from an evil conscience, and our bodies washed with pure water. Let us hold fast the profession [confession] of our faith without wavering; (for he is faithful that promised;)*
> *Hebrews 10:19–23*

The devil is a liar. You are perfectly redeemed. Hold fast your confession of the promise: "The blood of Jesus is stronger than the blood of my fathers! Old things (iniquity) are passed away. All things are become new."

The New Covenant reality tells us that Jesus Christ paid for iniquity, along with sin and transgression. Through the blood of Jesus, we have perfect redemption. 1 Corinthians 1:30 tells us that we have (past tense) redemption made unto us.

> But of him are ye in Christ Jesus, who of God is **made** unto us wisdom, and righteousness, and sanctification, and **redemption**.
>
> 1 Corinthians 1:30

Redemption is similar to righteousness and sanctification—they are given to us spiritually, but we must "walk them out" if we are going to receive the fullness of the gifts. The death of iniquity is accounted for in our gift of redemption, since it is included with the three wrongs that the blood of Jesus covers. We must claim these rights or they will be lost to the thief.

We are now ready to begin our study of how to apply the blood of Jesus. We have seen that His blood has been shed to pay for our acquittal. Now we need to apply the blood to claim our New Covenant rights. Rest assured that iniquity, sin, and transgression all died when we were born again.

As we learn how to apply the blood we will access, claim, and be able to walk in the freedom that Jesus purchased for us. Satan has no rights over you if you stand up and proclaim what Jesus Christ has done for you.

The blood of Jesus is stronger than the blood of my fathers!

PART FOUR

How to Apply
the Blood of Jesus

O ld Testament illustrations of the Passover and the Day of
Atonement clearly demonstrate that even though blood was
shed, it still needed to be applied. The blood of the
Passover lamb was applied to the doorposts and upper lintel, and
the blood of the goat was sprinkled before the mercy seat seven
times. The blood of the lamb profiles the three kinds of wrongs that
can be atoned, and the blood of the goat typifies the seven ways that
Jesus bled. In both cases, after the blood was shed, it had to be
applied.

This truth still is applicable in the New Testament. Jesus said in
Luke 22:20 that His blood, which was shed for you, was the New
Testament. Even though the blood was shed, it still needs to be
applied.

As we approach the broader topic of applying the blood, chapter 9
will discuss the specific way the blood needs to be applied — in faith
by confession. In chapter 10 we will discover that when His blood
is applied we access the ministry of Jesus Christ as the High Priest
of our confession. In chapter 11 we will cover in detail how to

apply the blood of Jesus so that we may receive the full benefit of the atonement. These aspects are closely interrelated and build upon each other.

All we have studied thus far directs us toward this point of practical implementation. Even though the blood of Jesus is just as strong and delivering today as it has been for 2,000 years, His blood *must be applied* in order to receive the full effect of its atoning power.

Chapter 9

The Connection Between Faith and Confession

Jesus Christ fulfilled the law by becoming the Passover Lamb (1 Corinthians 5:7); therefore, it is no longer necessary for us to physically sacrifice a lamb on the fourteenth of Nisan and strike its blood on a physical door. Now it is the blood of Jesus, shed nearly 2,000 years ago, that we need to apply today.

The Word of God is very clear as to how to apply His blood. The Old Testament hints of this fulfillment, but the New Testament is direct. It is not by slaying a goat or a lamb, but by confession!

> *If we **confess** our sins, he is faithful and just to forgive us our sins, and to cleanse us from all unrighteousness.*
>
> *1 John 1:9*

The way to apply the blood through confession was profiled on the Day of Atonement for New Testament fulfillment. The High Priest would lay his hands, which were stained by the blood of the scape-goat, on the live goat. He would then confess the iniquities, sins, and transgressions of the children of Israel over this live goat.

> *And Aaron shall lay both his hands upon the head of the live goat, and **confess** over him all the iniquities*

> *of the children of Israel, and all their transgressions*
> *in all their sins, putting them upon the head of the*
> *goat, and shall send him away by the hand of a fit*
> *man into the wilderness.*
>
> *Leviticus 16:21*

"To confess" must be clearly understood. It is the belief of some religious groups that confession means to tell something to a priest. Others believe it must be done privately at an altar; and still there are others who say it must be done publicly, either at a baptism or in a testimony. When we study the depth of the meaning of this word "confession," we will discover for ourselves its proper definition.

The Greek word for "confession" is *homologeo*. The etymology of this Greek word illustrates that its root word is from *logos*, a declaration. In other words, according to 1 John 1:9, we must actually say or declare something in order for the blood of Jesus to be applied. Whatever else we may learn, it is very clear we must speak forth what we need to be forgiven for. A further understanding of the prefix, *homo*, will give us additional insight.

The prefix *homo* means "like in substance, origin or function." When attached to the word *logos* or *logeo*, it means to say the same thing that the Word (*Logos*) of God says regarding the condition. This means when we apply the blood of Jesus, we are to state what the Word of God states about the sin, iniquity or transgression — that we have been wrong; we are guilty as charged — and the blood of Jesus was shed for our forgiveness.

Proper confession must include the stipulation required by the Word of God. The Bible does not say that we are required to confess to a religious leader, or at an altar, or in a public testimony. Although the confession may be made in those ways, the Bible declares that we only need to say it and mean it in our hearts. Confession simply means that we are to make a statement in accordance and agreement with the Word of God.

The Connection Between Faith and Confession

The undeniable fact remains that in order to apply the blood of Jesus to our sins, iniquities, and transgressions, we are to make a verbal proclamation of our guilt and the forgiveness the Lord offers. Our mouths, and the words that proceed from them, are manifestations of activities going on in our hearts, minds and wills. Jesus said that at judgment time, we absolutely shall give account of every word we speak (Matthew 12:36); therefore, we need to set a guard by the door of our mouths (Psalm 141:3 NKJ). We will be judged by the words we speak—they are the testimony of our lives.

There is a scribe angel that keeps account of all the things we say and do (Ecclesiastes 5:6). When we make a confession regarding the sins, iniquities, and transgressions we wish to be forgiven for, the angel makes a corresponding entry in our account ledger (Romans 14:10). Whether we make our confessions at the altar, with tears, in the presence of anyone or not, the angel records them. Then at the judgment, the account book will be opened and the angel and the Holy Spirit will be our witnesses in the presence of the Lord. (In the mouth of two witnesses, the truth is established.)

These confessions are often very emotional and may dispel years of grief and guilt. Tears and in-depth sorrow may accompany them; however, tears and sorrow are emotions, and as powerful as they are, they are not the standards of a confession. I have seen powerful emotional displays of confession only to see the individual go astray quickly after the emotion had subsided. I likewise have seen some confessions last long after the emotion left. The point is that it is not the emotion which validates the effectiveness of a confession—it is the faith that accompanies it.

Faith in confession is affirmed by a very noteworthy Scripture.

> *That if thou shalt **confess** with thy mouth the Lord Jesus, and shalt **believe** in thine heart that God hath raised him from the dead, thou shalt be saved. For with the heart man **believeth** unto righteousness; and with the mouth **confession** is made unto salvation.* Romans 10:9–10

In fulfilling the scriptural requirement for applying the blood of Jesus through confession, the prefix *homo* (earlier defined as "like in substance, origin, or function") asserts that the faith must simultaneously come out of your heart. In other words, there must be more than just speaking out—there must be "heart" behind it.

Observe what the Psalmist, David, said regarding confession and dealing with God.

> *Come and hear, all ye that fear God, and I will declare what he hath done for my soul. I cried unto him with my mouth, and he was extolled with my tongue.* **If I regard iniquity in my heart, the Lord will not hear me:** *But verily God hath heard me; he hath attended to the voice of my prayer. Blessed be God, which hath not turned away my prayer, nor his mercy from me.*
>
> *Psalm 66:16–20*

God deals with us in the same manner as good parents deal with their children. If a parent demands a child apologize for a wrong deed and the child responds with an obedient word but an insincere heart, it will not suffice. The parent says, "I hear what you are saying, but you don't mean it." God is like this too; we cannot fool Him. He requires that when you say something, you mean it. This includes being sorry for doing it and having the full intention of not doing it again. Be not deceived, God is not mocked (Galatians 6:7).

We have discussed the fact that the blood of Jesus must be applied in faith by confession. Next, we will see to whom the confession is made. How we apply the blood of Jesus is by confession with faith, but *to whom* we confess is to *the* High Priest. This involves the revelation of Jesus Christ as the High Priest of our Confession.

Chapter 10

The High Priest of Our Confession

If Christians were polled and asked the question, "What is Jesus Christ's job description right now?" the majority would respond, "Savior." This would be the correct response for someone actually being saved at the time, but technically, right now Jesus Christ is serving as High Priest, especially for those who are already saved. He is in the presence of God right now, on His knees, making supplication and intercession for you and me. He is our High Priest.

We need to learn how to access the Lord as our High Priest. As we do, we will discover how to apply His blood through confession.

> *Therefore, holy brethren, partakers of the heavenly calling, consider the Apostle and High Priest of our **confession**, Christ Jesus.*
>
> *Hebrews 3:1 NKJ*

> *But if we walk in the light, as he is in the light, we have fellowship one with another, and the blood of Jesus Christ his Son cleanseth us from all sin. If we **confess** our sins, he is faithful and just to forgive us our sins, and to cleanse us from all unrighteousness.*
>
> *1 John 1:7–9*

PERFECT REDEMPTION

Jesus Christ is the High Priest of our confession. He is the one who now makes intercession in the presence of God. As we confess our sins, iniquities, and transgressions before Him as our Redeemer, He intercedes for us in the very presence of God.

The book of Hebrews amplifies the revelation of Jesus Christ as our High Priest. Jesus Christ is referred to as our High Priest thirteen times, and it states that His function in heaven is to intercede for us. This revelation of our High Priest shows us that Jesus Christ is ever in the presence of God, and as we confess Jesus Christ, He confesses us before the Father.

> *For Christ [as our High Priest] is not entered the holy places made with hands, which are figures of the true, but into heaven itself, now to appear in the presence of God for us.*
>
> *Hebrews 9:24*

Jesus Christ, alone, is the only man who can make true intercession before God for our forgiveness. Overwhelming evidence from the Word of God reveals that we can only find access to the Father through His Son, Jesus Christ.

> *Jesus saith unto him, I am the way, the truth, and the life: no man cometh unto the Father, but by me.*
>
> *John 14:6*

> *For there is one God, and one mediator between God and men, the man Christ Jesus.*
>
> *1 Timothy 2:5*

Religion has far too long robbed the sincere Christian from a godly relationship with Jesus Christ as High Priest. We do not need Mary, or a vicar as an interceder to reach God, because we have a loving High Priest who can be touched with the depth of our infirmities.

> *Seeing then that we have a **great High Priest** who has passed through the heavens, Jesus the Son of God, let us hold fast **our confession**. For we do not*

The High Priest of Our Confession

have a High Priest who cannot sympathize with our
weaknesses, but was in all points tempted as we are,
yet without sin. Let us therefore come boldly to the
throne of grace, that we may obtain mercy and find
grace to help in time of need.

Hebrews 4:14–16 NKJ

We can come boldly before the Father because the blood of Jesus Christ was shed for us. The confession that we need to hold on to is what the Word of God confesses about us. We have forgiveness and access to the Father through our Lord Jesus Christ.

The Lord knows what it means to suffer; He even suffered when He was not guilty. He pleads our cause before the Father. He knows what it feels like to be physically hurt and to be rejected by others. He is a man well acquainted with grief. Surely He has borne our sorrows. We like sheep have gone astray, but the Father has laid on Jesus the iniquity of us all (Isaiah 53:4, 6). Jesus is our High Priest. We make confession of our sins, iniquities, and transgressions before Him, and He makes intercession before the Heavenly Father.

What goes on behind the scenes when an individual confesses their sins, iniquities and transgressions, and has applied the blood of Jesus, is revealed in the following verses. When we confess Jesus Christ on earth as our High Priest, Mediator, and Intercessor, He confesses us before the Father in heaven (Matthew 10:32). He likewise confesses us before the holy angels (Luke 12:8 and Revelation 3:5). When our sins, iniquities, and transgressions are forgiven, the Father, longing to show mercy, dispatches ministering spirits to you with His blessings (Hebrews 1:13–14, Ephesians 1:3, Psalm 20:1–2).

The ministry of Jesus Christ our High Priest brings us the favor of God, but it is only availed through confession. As we confess Him on earth, He confesses us in heaven and the covenant blessings are released.

PERFECT REDEMPTION

There is a breathtaking truth hidden in the Word of God concerning the closing of Jesus' earthly ministry as Prophet and the beginning of his heavenly ministry as High Priest. We can unveil this truth by comparing two verses of Scripture. They are Exodus 12:22 and John 19:29. Both of these verses illustrate the importance of applying the blood—one in the Old Covenant and one the New Covenant.

Understanding the background of these verses will enhance our appreciation for God's mercy and love. Both of these activities occurred at three o'clock on the fourteenth of Nisan. Jesus was crucified at exactly the same time the Passover lamb was slain. It is declared in 1 Corinthians 5:7 that Christ our Passover was sacrificed for us. He truly was our Passover.

As we look at the four common elements in Exodus 12:22 and John 19:29, remember that Jesus already told His disciples that His blood was shed to consecrate the New Covenant (Matthew 26:28, Mark 14:24, and Luke 22:20). Comparing these elements within these verses will disclose the ministry of our High Priest in a new light. The four elements are the blood, the basin, the hyssop, and the door.

> And ye shall take a bunch of **hyssop**, and dip it in the **blood** that is in the **bason**, and **strike the lintel and the two side posts** with the blood that is in the bason; and none of you shall go out at the door of his house until the morning.
>
> *Exodus 12:22*

> Now **a vessel** full of sour wine was sitting there; and they filled a sponge with sour **wine**, put it on **hyssop**, and put it to His **mouth**.
>
> *John 19:29 NKJ*

The bason relates to the vessel. The blood relates to the wine. Hyssop in both verses shows the "application of the blood." Where the blood was "applied" was to the door and to His mouth. This reveals a great truth regarding the close of Jesus' earthly ministry and the opening of His heavenly ministry as High Priest. The context of John 19:28 emphasizes that Jesus had one final thing to do before ending His earthly ministry. In order to accomplish it, He said with His mouth, "I thirst." He had to get the wine (blood) on His mouth (the door).

> *After this, Jesus, knowing that all things were now accomplished, that the Scripture might be fulfilled, said, "I thirst!"*
>
> *John 19:28 NKJ*

When Jesus said, "I thirst," they gave Him the wine, and when the wine touched His mouth, it was finished.

> *So when Jesus had received the sour wine, He said, "It is finished!" And bowing His head, He gave up His spirit.*
>
> *John 19:30 NKJ*

According to the Word of God, the very last thing Jesus had to do before He gave up His life was to get that wine on His mouth. This shows an incredible fulfillment. He then said, "It is finished." That which was finished was our redemption and His earthly ministry. With His earthly ministry finished, He was ready to begin His function as High Priest.

Comparing the door (where the blood was applied), and His mouth (where the New Testament consecration was applied), shows us His new ministry in heaven. The door, where the blood was applied, demonstrated protection from the wrath of God, as we saw earlier in Exodus 12:22, and also in Genesis 4:7. The Passover angel passed over the children of Israel because they were behind the door. Behind the door, they were safe. They were not supposed to go out until morning.

In the New Testament, under the new covenant, the protection we have from God's wrath is behind the door of the mouth of the Lord

Perfect Redemption

Jesus Christ. He is our High Priest who continually makes intercession for us before God. We are protected until the "morning" of the Day of the Lord when Jesus will no longer be before the mercy seat, but will sit upon the judgment seat.

> *But He, because He continues forever, has an unchangeable priesthood. Therefore He is also able to save to the uttermost those who come to God through Him, since He ever lives to make intercession for them. For such a High Priest was fitting for us, who is holy, harmless, undefiled, separate from sinners, and has become higher than the heavens.*
> *Hebrews 7:24–26 NKJ*

The mouth of the Lord Jesus Christ is now our protection from the wrath of God. The wine (which corresponds to the blood) was applied to His mouth. We are saved from the wrath of God because of His blood and His intercession.

> *Much more then, being now justified by his blood, we shall be saved from wrath through him.*
> *Romans 5:9*

Now the key to accessing Jesus Christ as our High Priest, and to being spared from the wrath of God—which is rightly and justly due us—is to apply the blood of Jesus by our confession. When we do, we stand behind the door of Jesus' confession before the Father.

> *Therefore, holy brethren, partakers of the heavenly calling, consider the Apostle and **High Priest of our confession**, Christ Jesus.*
> *Hebrews 3:1 NKJ*

As we apply the blood of Jesus, our High Priest, through confession to God, we should not be surprised to discover fountains of blessings overflowing from the Father of mercy and love. When we confess our sins, iniquities, and transgressions to God the Father, Jesus Christ, our faithful High Priest, shows the Father His hands, feet, back, side, brow, crown, and bruises. He is the faithful High Priest forever, who is continually making intercession for us before the Father.

The Father wants to give mercy. Because of the blood of Jesus, and the protection that His mouth as Intercessor offers, the Father can now legally grant us His mercy and forgiveness.

Having seen both Old and New Covenant realities of the blood, we are now ready to access our High Priest and apply the blood of Jesus through confession. After our confessions, we will stand behind the door, being protected by the intercession of our High Priest. Our confessions will be made to Jesus Christ, the Apostle and High Priest of our confession.

Neither by the blood of goats and calves, but by his own blood he entered in once into the holy place, having obtained eternal redemption for us.

Hebrews 9:12

Chapter 11

Applying the Blood of Jesus through Confession

W e have diligently studied about Jesus' shed blood to make our way to this point. Now it is time for practical application. Therefore, we need to understand exactly what we are to do in order to receive these wonderful blessings and covenant promises from God. Before getting to the "meat of the matter," where you will apply the blood of Jesus by making your confessions to Him, a little review will prepare you for this.

There can be no doubt regarding the fact of how we apply the blood of Jesus. We do not need to sacrifice a lamb, a bull, or a goat because Jesus already fulfilled these Old Covenant requirements. We are to apply His blood through confession. His blood was shed once and for all, and now we need to apply His blood to the door-post and lintel of our hearts for the forgiveness of sins, iniquities, and transgressions. Likewise, we need to acknowledge that the blood of Jesus was shed seven different ways in order to fully cleanse us of all our evil ways. Applying His blood can only be done through our confession.

As we do this, we can draw near to God with a heart full of assurance, because He who made the promises to us will fulfill them. The key is our confession with faith.

And having a High Priest over the house of God, let us draw near with a true heart in full assurance of faith, having our hearts sprinkled from an evil conscience and our bodies washed with pure water. **Let us hold fast the confession** *of our hope without wavering, for He who promised is faithful.*
Hebrews 10:21–23 NKJ

Confession, without a doubt, is how the blood of Jesus is applied. It accesses Him as our High Priest (Hebrews 3:1). This is how the High Priest removed the sins, iniquities, and transgressions of the people (Leviticus 16:21). It is how we receive the forgiveness of our wrongs and are cleansed from unrighteousness (1 John 1:7, 9). It is the key to entering into the covenant blessing of Abraham (Leviticus 26:42), and how we draw near to God to make a demand upon our faith, because He who promised is faithful (Hebrews 10:21–23).

The most defining and specific section of Scripture to instruct us regarding what God wants us to confess is Leviticus 26:40 and 41. These verses specifically state what we must confess in order for God to convey His covenant blessing of Abraham upon us. Now as we apply Jesus' blood through confession, we access His ministry as High Priest to make intercession for us before our Father.

Before we cover the details of our confession, we need to specify to whom we are to confess.

Confess to the High Priest

If you are Roman Catholic, or have come from a Roman Catholic background, you are probably familiar with going to confession. There is some certain validity in this action, but true confession is not made in a physical booth or to mortal men. Our confession is to be made in the temple of the Holy Spirit, within our own conscience, and to the only man qualified to offer intercession directly before the Father's throne—the Lord Jesus Christ, the High Priest

Applying the Blood of Jesus through Confession

of our confession.

Jesus Christ is the only way to God and He ever lives to make intercession for us (Hebrews 7:25).

> *Jesus said to him, "I am the way, the truth, and the life. No one comes to the Father except through Me.*
> *John 14:6 NKJ*

When we make our confession of the sins, iniquities, and transgressions we have committed, we confess them to Jesus Christ. He is the Lamb of God who takes away the sins of the world. The Lord Jesus is not only the High Priest, the offering, and the sacrifice, but also the only fit man able to take away all our sins, iniquities, and transgressions. He is all these things described in Leviticus 16:21.

> *And Aaron shall lay both his hands upon the head of the live goat, and confess over him all the iniquities of the children of Israel, and all their transgressions in all their sins, putting them upon the head of the goat, and shall send him away by the hand of a fit man into the wilderness:*
> *Leviticus 16:21*

The word "confess" means to say something (chapter 9) and that means we have a responsibility to actually open our mouths and make a statement. When we do, in a figurative sense, we are laying our hands on Jesus as the scapegoat to transfer our sin, iniquity, and transgressions to Him. We have accrued a debt that we cannot afford to pay.

The one to whom we make the statement, however, is to Jesus Christ our High Priest. Confession necessitates that you trust Him and trust in Him. He is alive and He is in the presence of the Father for this very reason. You must speak to Him in the privacy of your own heart and out of your own mouth by the volition of your own will. Jesus is our Advocate (1 John 2:1) and Mediator (1 Timothy 2:5). He is the one to whom we confess.

What You Need to Say

A great deal of what needs to be confessed is covered in Leviticus 26:40 and 41, but your specifics and details will need to come from the Holy Spirit. Jesus said that He would send us a Helper. This is the Holy Spirit.

> *"Nevertheless I tell you the truth. It is to your advantage that I go away; for if I do not go away, the Helper will not come to you; but if I depart, I will send Him to you.*
>
> *John 16:7 NKJ*

Verse 8 in John 16 shows how the Holy Spirit helps us. He tells us what to confess as He convicts us of sin.

> *"And when He has come, He will convict the world of sin, and of righteousness, and of judgment.*
>
> *John 16:8 NKJ*

We know that violating the written Scriptures and living contrary to them constitutes sin, but we also need to be aware that violating the inward convictions of the Holy Spirit is also sin, because now the law of God is written upon the tables of our heart. The general terms of our covenant with God are documented in the written agreement of the Bible, but the specific terms are qualified by the witness of the Holy Spirit.

When we confess our wrongs, the Holy Spirit bears witness with our spirit and with our conscience (Romans 8:16; 9:1). The Holy Spirit will be our witness at the judgment seat of Christ and will testify of our confessions, or lack of them, as the case may be. The Holy Spirit, accompanied by the scribe angel who is assigned to keep your account ledger (Ecclesiastes 5:6), will be the witnesses who will exonerate or convict you, based upon your confession and application of the blood of Jesus.

What the Holy Spirit has been working within you and witnessing to your conscience needs to be confessed. Specifics such as watching the wrong kind of movies, overeating, gossip, criticism, not paying your tithes, or not fulfilling your God-ordained calling need to be confessed. There may be sins of commission—what you have done wrong, and/or sins of omission—what you have not done. Realize that the Holy Spirit has been sent to help you through conviction, not to victimize you by condemnation. He wants to help you. It is the Father's good pleasure to give you His kingdom (Luke 12:32) and the Holy Spirit is here to help you confess the wrongs in your life. He is here to help prepare you to meet the Bridegroom by purging you so you may be dressed in a spotless wedding garment. A large part of our preparation is to confess the wrongs you have done and to change your lifestyle. The Lord wants to see your heart but He also wants to hear your words.

The areas you need to confess are those which have been an offense to God. The written Scriptures confirm it. Confess the lying, stealing, bearing false witness, unforgiveness, and other things the Word of God testifies of. These are the written words of the Holy Spirit (2 Peter 1:21). Also, confess those things the Holy Spirit has been witnessing to your conscience. It is your responsibility to open your mouth and speak as He leads you.

Purging Your Conscience by Applying Jesus' Blood to the Stain of Iniquity

Proverbs 16:6 gives us great information concerning how to apply the blood of Jesus through confession. It shows the blood shed and the blood applied and introduces us to the word "purged," the goal of God to set us free.

> *By mercy and truth iniquity is purged: and by the*
> *fear of the LORD men depart from evil.*
> *Proverbs 16:6*

Notice that iniquity is purged by mercy and truth. Mercy refers to the blood being shed, and truth refers to the blood being applied.

PERFECT REDEMPTION

Both are necessary. As potent as the blood of Jesus is, it is nonetheless ineffective until it is applied. This is similar to the blood of the Passover lamb that was caught in the basin. It did not protect the children of Israel until it was applied to the doorpost and the lintel. By mercy (the blood shed) and truth (the blood applied) iniquity is purged.

The word "purged" is a key concept in confessing our wrongs. "To purge" means a deep cleansing and it comes from the same root word as "pure." Purged is used throughout the Bible when dealing with the removal of stains and specifically the concept of iniquity.

> *How much more shall the blood of Christ, who through the eternal Spirit offered himself without spot to God, **purge** your conscience from dead works to serve the living God?*
>
> *Hebrews 9:14*

Our conscience is included within our spirit, and it is thoroughly cleansed by the blood of Jesus as we confess our iniquities. This confession will remove all vestiges and roots of dead works. These dead works will continue to re-emerge and reoccur until their cause is removed. But having shown that iniquity is the reason for continual sin and transgression, it becomes clear that by confessing the iniquity, the conscience can be purged.

The word "purge" is also related to "blotted out," another word to show deep cleansing and the removal of the residue of iniquity and the last traces of sin and transgression. The usage of this phrase in Colossians 2:14 shows the New Testament definition of iniquity and the removal of it.

> *And you, being dead in your sins and the uncircumcision of your flesh, hath he quickened together with him, having forgiven you all trespasses; **Blotting out** the handwriting of ordinances that was against us, which was contrary to us, and took it out of the way, nailing it to his cross.*
>
> *Colossians 2:13–14*

Applying the Blood of Jesus through Confession

Iniquity is the handwritten ordinance that was contrary to us. It was the generational charge that was against us. When the iniquity is blotted out is when sins and transgressions are purged. In other words, the stain of iniquity needs to be removed in order for the sin or trespass to be forgotten. Notice that sins and trespasses (transgressions) are removed when the iniquity is blotted out.

The foretold truth about the effect of having iniquity forgiven was shown in the prophecy of the New Covenant in Jeremiah 31:34. It reveals that when the iniquity is forgiven, the sin is then forgotten. (This verse is also quoted in Hebrews 8:12 and 10:17.)

> *And they shall [in the New Covenant] teach no more every man his neighbour, and every man his brother, saying, Know the LORD: for they shall all know me, from the least of them unto the greatest of them, saith the LORD:* **for I will forgive their iniquity, and I will remember their sin no more.**
> *Jeremiah 31:34*

The focal point is that when we confess our iniquity, Jesus' blood removes the stain that causes the sin, whether committed by us or by our ancestors. This confession removes the remembrance in the spirit realm of any generational cause whereby you could legally be charged. It is similar to doing laundry. When you have a stubborn stain, you put the detergent directly on the problem. Then, as the detergent removes the stain, it will clean the whole load of laundry while the stain is being removed. This is the salient point of understanding we need to glean from this study: **Confess the iniquity and the cause of the sin and transgression will be removed in the process.** Apply the blood directly to the iniquity and the stain will be removed. All trace and remembrance of the wrong is completely washed away.

Leviticus 26:40 and 41

Leviticus 26:40 and 41 are among the most important verses regarding this concentrated study. Remember these verses in order to help others when the Lord calls upon you to show them the path of freedom. They give us the proper direction concerning what we need to confess. Verse 42 confirms our actions. If we do this, then we receive that. If we confess, then the covenant blessing of Abraham will be given to us.

> *If they shall confess their iniquity, and the iniquity of their fathers, with their trespass which they trespassed against me, and that also they have walked contrary unto me; And that I also have walked contrary unto them, and have brought them into the land of their enemies; if then their uncircumcised hearts be humbled, and they then accept of the punishment of their iniquity:* **Then** *will I remember my covenant with Jacob, and also my covenant with Isaac, and also my covenant with Abraham will I remember; and I will remember the land.*
>
> *Leviticus 26:40–42*

The specifics of these verses are very important. The context reveals that the reason for captivity is because of iniquity and rebellion. Because of our father's transgressions, we were born into captivity. God demands that we confess our wrongs and the wrongs of our fathers if we are to be restored. Look at what Nehemiah says about confessing these things.

> *And the seed of Israel separated themselves from all strangers, and stood and* **confessed their sins, and the iniquities of their fathers.** *Nehemiah 9:2*

The children of Israel did not just confess their own sins, but the iniquities of their fathers, too. Daniel 9:5 and 6 show the same truth. The result of their confession was that God returned them to freedom. In the case of Israel, it was their land. In the New

Applying the Blood of Jesus through Confession

Testament sense, it is our liberty and freedom from the bondage of sins and transgressions.

In a moment, it will be time for you to pray and make your confession out of your mouth and out of your heart before the Lord, your High Priest. But before leading you in this prayer, I want to relate an actual occurrence that happened to me while teaching these same truths in India. This story demonstrates the need to handle rebellion head on and not to back down, because iniquity, as rebellion, could cause you to rebel against the very thing you need to do in order to be set free.

In sharing this account with you, I am handling any rebellion or "last ditch" efforts any evil spirit may offer to prevent you from doing what you must do. Rebellion is real, and iniquity is often manifested in a defiant attitude of "I am the exception and I don't need anybody telling me what to do." Let this story speak for itself and receive the exhortation and admonition of obedience that it is intended to show.

I was teaching in India about confessing to our High Priest when I noticed a man standing in the back of the room. His arms were folded across his chest in a defiant body posture, as if to say, "I don't believe anything you are saying." I spiritually perceived that he was in rebellion and that a demon was preventing him from being delivered. After the teaching, he "bulled" his way to the front of the class to confront me with his opinion. As he approached me, I must admit, I was more than ready to handle this head on. I wanted to see him delivered.

This man announced, "There is no such thing as iniquity and trans-gression. It is all sin and I do not need to confess anything. The blood was shed for me and I am clean." He looked at me through icy eyes of rebellion. The Holy Spirit came upon me as I locked gazes with him, much like the stare down between Paul and Elymas (Acts 13:8–9).

Perfect Redemption

I said, "I can prove to you that iniquity is real. Do you want me to?" Before he could respond, I continued, "It is a simple yes or no question. Do you want me to or not?" He reluctantly said, "Okay."

The Holy Spirit came upon me and gave me boldness and this word of knowledge. I said, "The proof that iniquity and rebellion are real is that you are *full* of them. The evidence that you have them is that your children do not like you because you are a tyrant. Your wife is afraid of you and does not like you because you never listen to her. You have never had any friends in your life because you would never listen to them, because you always had to be the boss. The three churches that have dismissed you have never liked you because your rebellion would not allow you to take any constructive criticism." (The gift of the word of knowledge certainly assisted me in regards to mentioning the three churches, and definitely helped me to confront this man.)

I continued by saying, "Not only have you never had any friends and your children and your wife do not like you, I don't like you either, because you are arrogant and hardheaded. Furthermore, more than me not liking you, God does not like you either, because He resists the proud but gives grace to the humble. And lastly, you do not like you because you are just like your Daddy, and you basically hated him because he acted just like you."

By this time, the man's defiant stare had turned into a slumping, stoop-shouldered conviction. He had the spiritual "swept-back" look, like people get from riding a motorcycle, from the impact of the words. I continued by saying, "Now that you know that iniquity and rebellion are real, you have two choices: either confess them and repent, or get out." By God's mercy and because of the conviction of the Holy Spirit, he repented and was delivered.

The point of this story is to confront any "last minute" whispers from the enemy. The devil fears the blood of Jesus—not in the basin, but on the doorposts; not in your mind, but coming out of your mouth. If the devil can control your tongue, he has the rudder of your ship. The tongue is the only muscle in the human body that

Applying the Blood of Jesus through Confession

is connected on only one end. Our responsibility is to connect the other end to the Holy Spirit and let Him lead.

Tell the devil now—**and say this out loud!** "Satan, shut up. I am in control of my life and I will confess what I want to confess."

Iniquity and rebellion are nasty problems. They were manifested in Cain in the form of "I am the exception." Please do not let these stiff-necked, stubborn traits keep you from confessing the following prayer and proclamation. Jesus shed His blood for you. Now it is time for you to step up to the plate and confess what the Holy Spirit leads you to confess.

Before we begin, I want to pray this prayer with you. This is not part of your confession, but I want you to ask the Holy Spirit to help you and reveal to you those things to confess when it is time for you to speak them out. Please say . . .

Holy Spirit, Jesus sent You to help me and I need Your help. The Word of God says in John 14:26 that You would bring things to my remembrance and in John 16:8 that You would convict me of sin. Please reveal to me those things I need to confess.

Now, I would like to lead you in this prayer and proclamation to confess the conditions in Leviticus 26:40 and 41. But first, I must be very firm regarding a specific issue at this point. These words you pray must be said out loud, not just read within your own mind. When it is time for you to confess what you need to say before your Lord and High Priest, remember, you are saying this to the man who was crucified for you and bled to death so you could be reconciled to God. You are not telling Him anything He does not already know, but He has been waiting for you to confess so that He can intercede for you before the Father.

Now say these things out loud—to the Lord Jesus Christ and to your Father God. Say these things out of your mouth and mean them in your heart.

Heavenly Father Yahweh and Lord Jesus Christ, my High Priest, I have sinned and come short of the glory of God. I have sins, iniquities, and transgressions for which I cannot pay. Lord Jesus, I lay my hands on You and ask You to take these away. I cannot pay for them. Father, these have been charged to me by Your righteous judgment for what my ancestors and I have done. By Your mercy, You have allowed my lineage to continue so that I could confess them before You.

Forgive me of my evil deeds and the wrong decisions I have made. Forgive me for following anything or anyone but Jesus and doing things that I have known were wrong. Forgive me for doubting You and remove the stain of my father's transgressions.

By my will and with my mouth, I freely confess that I have sinned and come short of Your glory. Lord Jesus, You are my High Priest and I confess before You the following deeds. I confess . . .

(Now be led by the Holy Spirit to confess what He has convicted you of, by what is written in the Scriptures or by what He has spoken to your conscience. Say this out loud. The scribe angel cannot read your mind and by your words, you will be justified— or by your words, you will be condemned.

Now continue, after you confess your wrongs, by saying to the Lord Jesus Christ, your High Priest.)

Lord Jesus Christ, You are my High Priest and I freely confess that my fathers have trespassed against You. They have rebelled against the commandments of God and have incurred Your wrath. They have shed innocent blood. They have committed immoral sexual acts. They have worshiped false gods and graven images, including themselves. They have profaned Your holy name and Your holy days. They have walked contrary to You but

by Your mercy, You put them, and me, in captivity instead of punishing them by death.

I recognize Your righteous judgment and that by Your mercy, You have let me live in captivity. I accept Your righteous judgment and ask You to forgive me for saying anything contrary to this. I am humble in my heart and accept that Your judgment has been righteous. Please forgive me of my sins, iniquities, and transgressions, and forgive my fathers for their sins and transgressions against You. Please return to me my freedom, and banish from me all accounts of the wrongs that we have committed.

I recognize that You alone are righteous and that only You—and You alone—can forgive me. Take these away from me.

Now, I accept the testimony of Your Word and proclaim, that I am righteous by the blood of Jesus. I have confessed my wrongs, and You are faithful and just to forgive me. You have cleansed me of all sin and unrighteousness. I have the righteousness of Jesus Christ by faith—not of my works, but by Your grace.

Father, I also, in Your presence, proclaim: I forgive myself. I forgive myself. By my own will, I forgive myself and decree that by the blood of Jesus Christ, I am forgiven. I proclaim that no evil spirits have any right over me because of the blood of Jesus. I rebuke them and command that they leave me and depart from my home, my presence, and me.

I accept the grace of God and Your forgiveness. I proclaim my righteousness by the love, grace, and mercy of God through the blood of Jesus Christ. I am forgiven of sins, transgressions, and iniquities. I am reconciled to God and receive my forgiveness and also my healing in my spirit, soul, and body.

Now that you have made these confessions and applied the blood of Jesus, you have a right to make a demand on your faith and expect the covenant you have made with God to be fulfilled.

> *And having a High Priest over the house of God, let us draw near with a true heart in full assurance of faith, having our hearts sprinkled from an evil conscience and our bodies washed with pure water. Let us hold fast the confession of our hope without wavering, for He who promised is faithful.*
>
> *Hebrews 10:21–23 NKJ*

Your confession was your first act of faith. Now, hold fast to your confession and expect to see the blessings of Abraham fulfilled in your life. By applying the blood of Jesus to your sins, iniquities, and transgressions, you have accessed the High Priest of your confession and have received forgiveness and the favor of God. The ministering spirits have been dispatched from the sanctuary. Be faithful. Your covenant blessing of Abraham is on its way to you.

Learning how to live redeemed will show you how to appropriate and keep the blessing God has given to you.

PART FIVE

Living Redeemed

B y applying the blood of Jesus, you have appropriated the same covenant blessings as were enjoyed by Adam and Abraham. By the grace of God, you are entitled to rights and privileges as a child of God. These are legal claims to your spiritual blessings and even though they are yours, faithful living is what you need to do to activate them.

Redemption is a gift of grace to you, but similar to the gifts of righteousness and sanctification (1 Corinthians 1:30), it must be walked out and claimed in everyday living. You will need to manage your mind and body by holding fast to your confessions that the old man is dead and you are a new creation in Christ Jesus. You will also need to handle the retaliation that comes from the devil. The devil is the accuser of the brethren and he will try his best to take these blessings away from you by lying to you and telling you that you still are not redeemed. You, however, have a legitimate right to claim your inheritance and to live a redeemed lifestyle, but it will require a concentrated effort.

This last portion of the book is designed to help you live in the covenant blessings that the grace of God has given you. These are short, practical keys to help you stay in the flow of God's blessing. These are lessons from the laboratory of life that have worked for many, many people for a long, long time. These will give you insight as to what to do in regards to changing your lifestyle, forgiving yourself, responding to accusation, and building an attitude of gratitude.

All of these are dependent upon you realizing and claiming what God has already done for you as a New Covenant reality and a new creation in Christ Jesus. All of the following chapters contain practical suggestions of confession. The new birth began by confessing Jesus as Lord and the practice necessary to claim the fullness of each of the promises is to confess them too. The last two chapters especially, "Offering the Sacrifice of Praise," and "Let the Redeemed of the Lord Say So" show this need for confession and give very practical advice and instruction for living redeemed.

Chapter 12

Depart from Iniquity

The Word of God is very clear that when entering into a covenant relationship with God, He expects you to live according to His standards. This is true in the Old Covenant as well as in the New. God does not change (Malachi 3:6 and Hebrews 1:12).

In the Old Testament, after the Passover was observed, the children of Israel entered into the Feast of Unleavened Bread, where God specifically told His children not to eat of any leavened bread. We shall see what this means to us as New Testament believers.

> *And the blood shall be to you for a token upon the houses where ye are: and when I see the blood, I will pass over you, and the plague shall not be upon you to destroy you, when I smite the land of Egypt. And this day shall be unto you for a memorial; and ye shall keep it a feast to the LORD throughout your generations; ye shall keep it a feast by an ordinance for ever. Seven days shall ye eat unleavened bread; even the first day ye shall put away leaven out of your houses: for whosoever eateth leavened bread from the first day until the seventh day, that soul shall be cut off from Israel.   Exodus 12:13–15*

PERFECT REDEMPTION

The New Testament gives us the same direction. The blood of Jesus is the token of our New Covenant. We are protected from the enemy and the wrath of God by the blood (Romans 5:9). We are to continue living in this covenant by spiritually keeping the feast of unleavened bread—to depart from the evil thing.

> *Purge out therefore the old leaven, that ye may be a new lump, as ye are unleavened. For even Christ our passover is sacrificed for us:* **Therefore let us keep the feast**, *not with old leaven, neither with the leaven of malice and wickedness; but with the unleavened bread of sincerity and truth.*
> *1 Corinthians 5:7–8*

The New Testament application of the Old Testament truth of keeping the feast means to change our lifestyle and remove the leaven of our old ways of living. We are to walk in sincerity and truth. These words, sincerity and truth, give us the criterion we must abide in to maintain our covenant with God.

Truth is to walk by the mandates of the written Word of God. Jesus said in John 17:17 that "Thy word is truth." We must live by the written Scriptures. This keeps our souls in obedience to God (James 1:21) and our lives in flow with the blessings of God. We have already seen that the translation of iniquity is "lawlessness" and it is often manifested by an attitude of "I am the exception." In living redeemed we must accept the covenant requirements and come apart from the accursed things. (See Joshua, chapters 6 and 7.) We must live by the commandments of the Bible.

Walking in sincerity is simply being led by the Holy Spirit. The written Word of God gives the general guidelines for obedience and covenant living, but the Holy Spirit gives the specifics. The word for sincerity means "to be judged by the light." The light of the Holy Spirit shines on everything we do. We need to be sensitive to the leading of the Holy Spirit. Remember that Jesus sent Him to help us, and that following Him will lead us into righteousness and true holiness.

Depart from Iniquity

There is another exhortation that instructs us in the same manner.

> *Nevertheless the foundation of God standeth sure, having this seal, The Lord knoweth them that are his. And, Let every one that nameth the name of Christ* **depart from iniquity**.
>
> *2 Timothy 2:19*

The context of both 1 Corinthians 5:7–8 and 2 Timothy 2:19 is to come apart from those individuals of the wrong influence. The Bible tells us in 2 Timothy 2:20 and 21 to purge ourselves from vessels of dishonor. This means to not keep company with evil people who walk in opposition to the Word of God and His holiness. This does not imply we should never witness to them, but as a child of God, we should not have a full fellowship with them.

Perhaps your mother told you what my mother told me: "It's not what you do, but the company you keep." Or in another cliché, "If you wallow with dogs, you will come out with fleas." My mother told me these things when I first made the decision to live a Christian life. I was living with some of my old "cronies" and they were continually tempting me with the old way of living. They were even belittling me for the way I believed. I thought it was my responsibility to witness to them. What I found out was this—they were witnessing to me too, but their witness was keeping me in sin and offense before God. I moved out and left them behind. I came apart from the very thing that was holding me down and holding me back. I don't know where they are now, but I followed "the Way" and left them behind.

The exhortation is clear and the commandment of God is firm. For you to live redeemed, let everyone that names the name of Christ depart from iniquity. Leave the past behind—like the children of Israel did when they crossed the Red Sea. Don't keep company with unclean things. You will not make them clean—they will only contaminate you.

PERFECT REDEMPTION

Keep company with those individuals who live in the light and walk in holiness. And always remember, "Evil company corrupts good habits," (1 Corinthians 15:33 NKJ).

To live redeemed, depart from iniquity and the influence of it!

Chapter 13

Forgive Yourself

Over the years, the issue of forgiving yourself continues to plague people even after God has forgiven them. Perhaps this results from continually seeing the consequences that have occurred due to a sin, iniquity, or transgression; or maybe it is their guilt from what has happened before. There are two basic reasons why people have difficulty forgiving themselves: (1) they must manage and discipline their own minds, (2) they must deal with evil spirits who remind them of their offenses.

Forgiveness is a decision of the will—it is not an emotion. Jesus said in Matthew 18:35 that forgiveness is from the heart, not the mind. We must therefore stand firm on the decision that is made.

The mind is subservient to the spirit and is manageable, and we can live from the spirit base and not the mind. The spirit of man is quickened and made mighty by the Holy Spirit. Now, after being regenerated by the Holy Spirit (Titus 3:5), we can dominate our mind by our spirit, which is superior in might and authority. We are told by 2 Corinthians 10:5 to cast down imaginations and to bring captive every thought to the obedience of Christ. Luke 21:19 also indicates, "In your patience, possess ye your souls." These things can be done if the spirit rules over the mind and soul. You must be tough on your mind by living with a strong spirit.

Managing the mind deals with deep issues, but the Bible is clear that the mind *can* be renewed.

> *And do not be conformed to this world, but be trans-formed by the renewing of your mind, that you may prove what is that good and acceptable and perfect will of God.*
>
> *Romans 12:2 NKJ*

A good friend of mine, Rev. Tom Sexauer from San Antonio, Texas, has ministered to people for many years and instructs them to say this: "I forgive myself, I forgive myself, I will to forgive myself." Have you done this? Have you made this decision? Have you taken a stand to walk in His light or are you continuing to wallow in self-pity and shame? Unless you consciously make the decision to forgive yourself, your mind will not have been told how to behave.

Once you have made the decision to forgive yourself, you must enforce it by bringing every thought captive to the obedience of Christ. You may need to speak out loud to your mind and say, "I have forgiven myself and I am cleansed by the blood of Jesus. Now, mind, shut up and be renewed according to the Word of God. I have made the decision to forgive myself, and I will live by my decisions and my will instead of my emotions." Then quote Bible verses from memory. Say, "It is written . . ."

The next problem of not forgiving ourselves is not in dealing with just our mind and memories, but with demons or evil spirits who accuse us. This is also a deep issue, but fundamentally the solution lies in knowing that you have authority over evil spirits.

> *"Behold, I give you the authority to trample on ser-pents and scorpions, and over all the power of the enemy, and nothing shall by any means hurt you."*
>
> *Luke 10:19 NKJ*

There are two things you must do regarding these evil spirits. First, you must recognize that you are not the one thinking these thoughts of unforgiveness, but you are listening to them speaking to you in the spirit realm. After you realize this, then secondly, you must *verbally* rebuke them.

You are a spirit being, and as such, you can distinguish between the soul and the spirit (Hebrews 4:12). There is a spirit realm and you actually are in touch with it. Many people are walking around listening to demons, believing that they are actually thinking those terrible thoughts. Generally, when Christians are plagued with recurring thoughts that are contrary to the Word of God, it is because evil spirits are talking to them. It is not because the person is evil or truly thinking these things.

When you realize that evil spirits speak to you and accuse you of sins, iniquities, or transgressions that you have been forgiven for, you must verbally respond to them. Evil spirits cannot read your thoughts, but they can put them in your spirit by speaking and making suggestions to you. You must retaliate out loud! We are thankful they cannot read our minds; however, this means we also cannot "think" them out of our lives.

I cannot begin to tell you how many people I have seen delivered almost overnight when they realized this truth. On the other hand, I have seen lots of people forget this lesson, internalize the conversation, and get beaten up by demons. My heart cries out, "In the name of God, man, speak out and speak up! Take control over the spirit of retaliation by retaliation." You have the bigger gun. Pull the trigger. Get control of your muzzle.

You can rebuke evil spirits. They may return and you may have to do it again (like you would with a pesky salesman), but you *do* have authority over them. If you chase them away consistently, they will finally learn.

So in order to forgive yourself, you must manage your mind according to the decision you have made and make it obey. As evil spirits start their accusations, you must verbally rebuke them and drive them away. Do just as Jesus did to Satan in the wilderness, command them to, "Get thee hence," (see Matthew 4:10). You have authority over them by the blood of Jesus and in His name.

As you continue to stay faithful in these matters, your mind can be re-educated—and the evil spirits will learn, too. Remember to stay faithful. Habits are formed through use: the old ones were and new ones can be too. Use your new habits of authority to break the old ones of defeat. The Holy Spirit is your Helper. He will give you the strength and spiritual insight to overcome this problem. Become sensitive to Him. He is your Helper and will remind you to live as a spirit being, to manage your mind and emotions, and to confront the evil spirits who speak to you.

To forgive yourself, live as a spirit being. Control your mind and your muzzle.

Chapter 14

Learn How to Behave in the Courtroom of Justification

The Bible uses many metaphors to describe the heavenly and spiritual realities going on around us. It uses vineyards, wedding ceremonies, temples, and in a related sense, the courtroom of God. In learning how to live redeemed it is necessary to understand how to behave in this courtroom of justification.

The characters and the stage of the courtroom must first be set. God the Father is Judge and is seated on the throne. There are other characters, the accusation, and of course the verdict.

> *"I watched till thrones were put in place, and the Ancient of Days [God the Father] was seated; His garment was white as snow, and the hair of His head was like pure wool. His throne was a fiery flame, Its wheels a burning fire; A fiery stream issued And came forth from before Him. A thousand thousands ministered to Him; Ten thousand times ten thousand stood before Him. The court was seated, And the books were opened."*
>
> *Daniel 7:9–10 NKJ*

You are on trial and the books that are opened before Him give evidence of your life and activities. The Holy Spirit is your witness (Romans 8:16 and 9:1; Hebrews 10:15) and the scribe angel who made the entries in the book (Ecclesiastes 5:6) is present also.

Facing you is the prosecuting attorney, Satan—the accuser. (He is called the accuser in Job chapters 1 and 2, and in Revelation 12:10.) He is charging you with unrighteousness.

> *Oh, that I had one to hear me! Here is my mark. Oh, that the Almighty would answer me, that my Prosecutor [Satan] had written a book!*
> *Job 31:35 NKJ*

You are seated in the courtroom, facing the Judge. The accuser reads the charges before His throne. Do not despair even though you are facing blatant facts of guilt. Seated next to you is your defense attorney, your Advocate, Jesus Christ the righteous.

> *My little children, these things I write to you, that you may not sin. And if anyone sins, we have an Advocate [defense attorney] with the Father, Jesus Christ the righteous.*
> *1 John 2:1 NKJ*

As the charges are read, you look down at your hands and realize that they are the culprits and have been instruments of unrighteousness. But then, as you glance over and see the hands of your defense attorney, you see the deep scars where nails pierced His hands. Where despair and certain conviction has ruled your mind, now the hope of righteousness rests "in His hands."

As the prosecutor reads the charges, the Holy Spirit and the scribe angel open the book. Sure enough, the charges are valid. Maybe the charge is theft, or a sexual sin, or lying, or anger, or pride, ad infinitum. The question is, "How do you plead?"

The nominal Christian may simply hang his head, waiting for the Judge to pass the verdict. Perhaps a more informed Christian may stand up to face his accuser and proclaim his innocence, even by the blood of Jesus. But the one who knows how to behave in the courtroom of justification will look to Jesus, the author and finisher of our faith.

Yes, we may want to stand up and defend ourselves. We may want to explain all the details and mitigating circumstances and why we did what we did. But you are not licensed to practice law in this courtroom. The old barrister's saying applies here: "The man that represents himself in court has a fool for a client and an imbecile for an attorney."

Here is how you behave in the courtroom of justification: Trust the Lord Jesus Christ. Let Him defend you.

The Lord stands up and declares, "My client pleads guilty."

> *"Agree with your adversary quickly, while you are on the way with him, lest your adversary deliver you to the judge, the judge hand you over to the officer, and you are thrown into prison."*
>
> *Matthew 5:25 NKJ*

The Lord Jesus Christ turns to the Holy Spirit and the scribe angel and says, "Here are the witnesses to verify the guilt." As the angel opens the book to the pages listing the sins, iniquities and transgressions, the Holy Spirit says, "We had these offenses listed, but they have been blotted out."

> *And you, being dead in your sins and the uncircumcision of your flesh, hath he quickened together with him, having forgiven you all trespasses; Blotting out the handwriting of ordinances that was against us, which was contrary to us, and took it out of the way, nailing it to his cross.*
>
> *Colossians 2:13–14*

Jesus then speaks, "Father, I have paid for these offenses. My client is guilty as charged, but I paid the penalty." He holds up His hands and then lifts His hair from his forehead revealing the deep puncture wounds from the crown of thorns. He then turns around and shows the stripes on His back.

The courtroom becomes silent as the Ancient of Days lifts His white, woolly head and stares at you through His fiery red eyes of wrath. His eyes then turn to soft compassion as He speaks, "My desire has always been mercy and compassion for you. By the blood and sacrifice of Jesus, you have been saved from My wrath."

> *Much more then, being now justified by his blood,*
> *we shall be saved from wrath through him.*
> *Romans 5:9*

He lifts His gavel to pronounce judgment and announces, "Let the record and the books show that my decree is—*justified*!"

> *Therefore being justified by faith, we have peace*
> *with God through our Lord Jesus Christ.*
> *Romans 5:1*

"Justified" in a word-related sense means "just as if I'd" never sinned. You are completely justified by the blood of Jesus.

This calls to mind a dream that came to the famous reformer, Martin Luther, when he was similarly accused by Satan. I offer a paraphrase of the recounted dream: "One night, Satan appeared at the foot of my bed and unrolled a scroll with all my sins written on it. There was no denying the facts. I broke out into a cold sweat as the devil continued to charge me with guilt. Then suddenly, appearing at the other bed post, was the Lord Jesus Christ. He instructed me to command the devil to unroll the whole scroll. When I did, as the last line of the scroll was unrolled, I saw written in blood red ink, 'Paid for in full by the Lord Jesus Christ.' The devil disappeared from before me," and he will disappear from before you too, if you let Jesus and His blood be your testimony and defense.

Learn How to Behave in the Courtroom of Justification

It is not necessary to defend yourself in the courtroom of justification. Many people try to only because they have not learned to trust their Advocate, Jesus Christ the righteous.

To continue the story line of the courtroom of justification, after you hug God and your Attorney, and rejoice over the victory, you turn to walk out of the courtroom. Standing face to face with you is Satan, the prosecutor. Through clenched teeth and with hatred in his voice, he says, "You know that you are guilty."

With confidence in your voice and without blinking your eye, you stare back at him and assert with a calm force, "Shut up, devil. Go talk to my attorney."

That is how you behave in the courtroom of justification. Do not defend yourself. The blood of Jesus speaks for you. If you need to say anything at all, tell the devil to talk to your attorney.

Although this "courtroom" may seem like a contrived scenario, the reality does exist. If you will learn to live redeemed by agreeing quickly with your adversary and sending him to talk to Jesus when he accuses you, the devil will soon leave you alone. I have received testimony after testimony regarding the effectiveness of this tactic.

A lady once shared with me that a demon would continually come to her and accuse her of something from deep in her past. Even after confessing her sins, iniquities, and transgressions, she was confronted by whisperings from the defeated demon. She said, "I was washing dishes and this evil spirit said to me, 'You're really not forgiven. See, you still have guilt'." Upon hearing these words and remembering how to behave in the courtroom of justification, she said, "Shut up liar. Go talk to my attorney." That evil spirit has not been back!"

Remember your Advocate is Jesus Christ the righteous. You are not righteous by your works, but only by the blood of Jesus Christ. If you need to say anything at all, simply assert, "Shut up, devil. Go talk to my attorney." That is how to behave in the courtroom of justification.

Chapter 15

Cleanse Your Generational Line

Parents are understandably concerned regarding the iniquitous condition of their children. Because iniquity is passed down through the generations (Exodus 34:7 and 20:5) many people frequently ask, "Now that I am forgiven of my iniquity, are my children free from it too?" This is a serious matter that needs to be addressed.

It is necessary to understand and apply what the Bible teaches in regards to this subject. God's Word states that iniquity is passed down at the time of conception.

> *Behold, I was shapen in iniquity; and in sin did my mother conceive me.*
>
> *Psalm 51:5*

This verse clearly tells us that children have a pre-molded shape at the time of conception. The fact that iniquity is passed down to the "generations" indicates that it comes through the genes. This fact reveals many things about a child's character and about the "direction" they grow. It is their genetic "bent."

It would be a wonderful thing to tell people that when they confessed their iniquities that their children would be cleaned up in the process. Unfortunately, it would not be true. When the gene code was constructed, the old saying applies, "The die is cast." The fact is clear: if unreconciled iniquities were resident within you at the time of your child's conception, there is a good possibility these iniquities were passed on.

> *I the LORD thy God am a jealous God, visiting the iniquity of the fathers upon the children unto the third and fourth generation of them that hate me; And shewing mercy unto thousands of them that love me, and keep my commandments.*
>
> *Exodus20:5b–6*

We need to balance this discussion with an understanding that blessings transmit for thousands of generations, but iniquity for only three or four. It is a natural tendency to focus on what needs to be fixed, rather than to see what is already okay. Do not be in such a state of concern that you fail to see the good in your child and focus only on the bad.

If your child was "shapen" or conceived in iniquity, they need to do exactly what you did. They need to apply the blood of Jesus to receive their forgiveness. Otherwise they (like you) may continue to bear the propensity and tendency in their gene code. However, if your children are taught about their pitfalls and tendencies, and especially if they are taught about applying the blood of Jesus, it will be much easier for them to subdue their innate desires and dispositions.

The same truth applies to adopted children. It would be nice to say that when a paper was signed that gene codes were changed, but this would not be true, either. Saying that would be a disservice to both the parents and the children. Adopted children need careful instruction and usually greater focus upon handling the innate tendencies of iniquity because of the rejection most of them have experienced since the womb. They need to be taught about their iniquities and the power of the blood of Jesus.

*Therefore shall ye lay up these my words in your heart and in your soul, and bind them for a sign upon your hand, that they may be as frontlets between your eyes. And ye shall **teach** them your children, speaking of them when thou sittest in thine house, and when thou walkest by the way, when thou liest down, and when thou risest up. And thou shalt write them upon the door posts of thine house, and upon thy gates: That your days may be multiplied, and the days of your children, in the land which the LORD sware unto your fathers to give them, as the days of heaven upon the earth.*

Deuteronomy 11:18–21

The commandment of the Lord is to teach the children. This instruction needs to include their heritage, what God has called them to be, as well as potential pitfalls along the way. I told my children about the iniquity in my lineage and what I had possibly passed along to them. Then I warned them what to watch out for, and to be prepared for what the devil might throw at them. I told my children by painting a mind picture for them. I said, "Picture yourself walking in a minefield. Each step could spell disaster. But now, through an understanding of iniquity, each mine has a red flag sticking out of the ground, marking its location. On each flag is written the *iniquity*. Don't go there!"

If children are instructed regarding the blood of Jesus, and if they do not commit transgressions similar to those of their ancestors, then their children will not bear iniquity. If you are not a parent yet, there is good news. The iniquitous traits and tendencies from your side of the family have been put under the blood and now will *not* show up in your children.

Remember that the blood of Jesus was not only shed for the forgiveness of sins, iniquities, and transgressions, but also to strengthen us in the areas where we are weak. Likewise, we should expect to produce a lineage of children superior to ourselves because of the blessings of the Lord and the reversal of the curse by the blood of Jesus.

Chapter 16

Take Communion (Properly)

The whole New Covenant, based upon the blood of Jesus, was instituted at the time of the Last Supper. For us to live redeemed, we must remember the significance of the shedding of the Lord's blood and the sacrifice of His body.

> *And he took bread, and gave thanks, and brake it, and gave unto them, saying, This is my body which is given for you: this do in remembrance of me. Likewise also the cup after supper, saying, This cup is the new testament in my blood, which is shed for you.*
>
> *Luke 22:19–20*

The Old Covenant profiled this reality through the events of the Passover (Exodus 12). The lamb was separated, slain, and the blood was struck on the doorposts of each home on the fourteenth of Nisan. They ate the flesh of the lamb. The wine and bread that Jesus shared with His disciples revealed the greater reality that Passover represented. Jesus Christ is the true Passover.

> *Purge out therefore the old leaven, that ye may be a new lump, as ye are unleavened. For even **Christ our passover** is sacrificed for us.*
>
> *1 Corinthians 5:7*

PERFECT REDEMPTION

The New Covenant was instituted by the Lord Jesus Christ just before He died. Knowing that He would become the sacrificial lamb on the fourteenth of Nisan, Jesus gave the disciples specific instructions about what to do to commemorate His life, death, and accomplishments. These same commandments were emphatically restated by the Apostle Paul.

> *For I have received of the Lord that which also I delivered unto you, That the Lord Jesus the same night in which he was betrayed took bread: And when he had given thanks, he brake it, and said, Take, eat: this is my body, which is broken for you: this do in remembrance of me. After the same manner also he took the cup, when he had supped, saying, This cup is the new testament in my blood: this do ye, as oft as ye drink it, in remembrance of me.*
>
> *1 Corinthians 11:23–25*

The importance of taking communion is firmly stated in verse 26.

> *For as often as ye eat this bread, and drink this cup, ye do shew the Lord's death till he come.*
>
> *1 Corinthians 11:26*

This verse instructs all Christian believers that they may take the elements of communion as often as they choose and when they do, it is to remind them of the significance of the Lord's death.

The importance of partaking in communion correctly is firmly stated in verse 27. This verse introduces a section of Scripture that receives relatively little attention in most Christian circles.

> *Wherefore whosoever shall eat this bread, and drink this cup of the Lord, unworthily, shall be guilty of the body and blood of the Lord.*
>
> *1 Corinthians 11:27*

Take Communion (Properly)

It is a scary thing to say, but individuals who have been taking communion without knowledge of how the Lord bled, what His blood was shed for, and where to apply the blood of Jesus have been unwittingly defaming the sacrifice of the Lord Jesus Christ.

The word "unworthy" is the Greek word *anaxios*. This comes from the root word *axios*, which means to weigh an item on a scale of balances. The prefix *an* means "without." Literally, the word unworthily, in regards to taking communion, means "to not weigh out the significance of the Lord's death and balance it with living a corresponding lifestyle." This is a very serious matter and the Word of God is neither silent nor ambiguous about the consequences of taking the Lord's sacrifice for granted.

> *But let a man examine himself, and so let him eat of that bread, and drink of that cup. For he that eateth and drinketh unworthily, eateth and drinketh damnation to himself, not discerning the Lord's body. For this cause many are weak and sickly among you, and many sleep.*
>
> *1 Corinthians 11:28–30*

We need to examine ourselves when taking communion. We need to recognize the significance of the Lord's death by remembering the seven ways Jesus bled. We need to remember that He shed the blood out of His hands for our deeds to be forgiven; out of His feet for our wrong decisions and shame; out of His back for our healing; out of His crown for our idolatry; out of His side for our rebellion; out of His brow for our weak-mindedness and not praying enough; and where He was bruised, it was for our iniquities.

Verse 29 says that we are to discern the Lord's body. Discern is the Greek word *diakrino*. Strong's #1252 defines this as "to separate and make a distinction." What does it mean when it says to separate the Lord's body and to consider the distinction of it? Some have said to consider the members of the body of Christ and the importance of each of them. Even though this is a good idea, this is not the context of chapter 11 of 1 Corinthians. We are dealing with taking communion in an unworthy manner. We must separate and consider each part of the Lord's body, the way He bled, why He bled in that way, and the significance of the blood that came out of His body in that place. We must furthermore apply that blood for our forgiveness and to reverse the curse on us.

This is the significance of communion. The Word of God could not be more accurate when it testifies that if we do not examine ourselves properly when taking communion, we get "sick and die prematurely." This is not a game or a religious club. Your very life depends upon obeying this Word.

Do not read past this exhortation and treat it as just another "good idea." We are dealing with recognizing why Jesus bled and died for you. Verses 28–30 say that if we do not examine ourselves and take communion by weighing out the significance of the Lord's sacrifice and death, then this is the cause of many being sick and dying prematurely. I beg you, for the sake of the Lord's heart and love for you, and for the sake of your health and life—not to mention your whole family—please give this matter your wholehearted attention, in understanding this and applying it.

When we take communion we are re-committing our trust in our High Priest. We call to remembrance all the ways that Jesus bled and we apply that blood by our confession of sins, iniquities, and transgressions to the High Priest. We remember that Jesus loved us so much that He died for us to be reconciled to God.

Discern the Lord's body by taking communion properly!

Chapter 17

Offer the Sacrifice of Praise

Not only does the Old Testament give us profiles concerning the blood that Jesus shed and how to apply it, but it also provides us direction about what to do after we are forgiven. We offer our sacrifice of praise.

Following the Day of Atonement, when the High Priest sprinkled the blood seven times and confessed the sins, iniquities, and transgressions of the children of Israel over the live goat, the whole nation began a celebration—a feast of the Lord called the Feast of Tabernacles.

> *Speak unto the children of Israel, saying, The fifteenth day of this seventh month shall be the feast of tabernacles for seven days unto the LORD.*
>
> *Leviticus 23:34*

This feast was a reminder to the children of Israel that God brought them out of bondage and gave them a home. As a reminder of His deliverance, they lived in a booth, tent, or tabernacle for seven days. This reminded them of the captivity from which they had been freed. For each of those seven days, the children of Israel were supposed to give an offering to the Lord to demonstrate their thankfulness for having a home and being free

> *Seven days ye shall offer an offering made by fire*
> *unto the LORD: on the eighth day shall be an holy*
> *convocation unto you; and ye shall offer an offering*
> *made by fire unto the LORD: it is a solemn assem-*
> *bly; and ye shall do no servile work therein.*
>
> *Leviticus 23:36*

These offerings were a special way to say thank you to the Lord for His deliverance for them (Leviticus 23:37). Likewise, we need to spiritually keep this feast and offer our offerings of thankfulness for being set free and delivered out of the bondage of sin, iniquity, and transgression.

The offering we give to the Lord, however, is not one involving a lamb, goat, drink, flour, or incense, but an offering of praise.

> *By him therefore let us offer the sacrifice of praise*
> *to God continually, that is, the fruit of our lips*
> *giving thanks to his name.*
>
> *Hebrews 13:15*

This is instruction on how to live redeemed after you have confessed before the Lord and received your freedom. I am asking you now to continue your deliverance by keeping this feast in your heart. Can you make a commitment to offer a sacrifice of praise to God every day for at least a week? Will you do this?

Every day for the next week, around the time of the evening sacrifice (at about sunset), go out and offer Him your offering. Lift your hands to the heavens, lift your voice in praise and bless the Lord for His gift of freedom to you. When you do, it will please the Lord to see your attitude of gratitude.

> *But to do good and to communicate forget not: for*
> *with such sacrifices God is well pleased.*
>
> *Hebrews 13:16*

In Luke 17:12–18, Jesus ministered healing to ten lepers. Ten were healed but only one returned to say thank you. Will you be one of the nine or will you be the one who will come back to give thanks? The Lord notices now, even as He did then.

There is a verse of Scripture from the book of Revelation that should speak loudly to all of us. It reveals how we can overcome Satan, and it demonstrates how offering a sacrifice of praise is the only perfect response for the gift of freedom that the blood of Jesus has given us.

> *And they overcame him [Satan] by the blood of the*
> *Lamb, and by the word of their testimony; and they*
> *loved not their lives unto the death.*
> *Revelation 12:11*

When you begin to offer the sacrifice of praise to the Lord for what the blood of Jesus has done, you begin building the word of your testimony. Whatever God has delivered you from—alcoholism, homosexuality, lying, fear, et cetera—lift up your voice and praise Him for it. As you praise Him, you are preparing yourself for the next action—overcoming Satan.

Some day, maybe when you are not expecting it, God is going to call on you to be a witness for Him. You may not know a lot of Bible verses, nor be a professional speaker, but the one thing you do know (and are an expert on) is what God has done for you. One day, the Holy Spirit will ask you to tell someone what you have been delivered from. When He does, because you have praised the Lord for it and have been confessing your deliverance, you will be ready.

You will walk up to that person and say, "The Lord wants me to tell you what He has done for me." The Holy Spirit will lead you to testify to people and your testimony will win them for the Lord. The old adage applies here—the best testimony is a satisfied customer.

Jesus did not come just to save you and get you out of the pit of despair. He also came to reinstate you to the position from which

Adam fell. He did not save you just so you could sit and warm a church pew, but to stand, step out, and be a witness for Him.

> *How much more shall the blood of Christ, who through the eternal Spirit offered himself without spot to God, purge your conscience from dead works* **to serve the living God?**
>
> *Hebrews 9:14*

The Lord purchased you by redemption to be zealous for good works.

> *Who gave himself for us, that he might redeem us from all iniquity, and purify unto himself a peculiar people, zealous of good works.*
>
> *Titus 2:14*

When you offer the sacrifice of praise to the Lord not only are you preparing yourself to give the word of your testimony, but also every time you offer praise, you increase the distance between you and the demons who used to torment you.

Let us pray together, give thanks, and proclaim all that our Lord has done for us. This is an example of the proclamation you will be making this evening and for the rest of the week.

I freely offer the sacrifice of praise with my lips, giving thanks unto Your name. I thank You, Lord, for Your life and Your blood that You shed for me. I accept Your sacrifice with thankfulness and bless Your name for Your goodness. Use me, Lord, to build Your kingdom and open doors of utterance for me to speak of Your love, gentleness, goodness, and forgiveness.

Dear Lord, thank You for the blood that You shed as You bled seven different ways. I thank You for the forgiveness of my sins, iniquities, and transgressions that You took away.

I thank You, Lord, that You have given me a testimony of how good and merciful You are. I bless You and thank You for perfect redemption and a hope of eternal inheritance that fades not away.

Offer your sacrifice of praise like the children of Israel did when they were delivered and forgiven. Do this every afternoon for a week. It most likely will become a great habit in your life—to praise the Lord from the rising of the sun to the going down of the same.

> *For from the rising of the sun even unto the going down of the same my name shall be great among the Gentiles; and in every place incense shall be offered unto my name, and a pure offering: for my name shall be great among the heathen, saith the LORD of hosts.*
>
> *Malachi 1:11*

Properly confessing the realities of the Word of God is the only way you can live above iniquity and the lies of the world.

Chapter 18

Let the Redeemed
of the Lord Say So

A re you redeemed by the Lord? Have you been redeemed from the hand of the enemy? If so, then say so.

Let the redeemed of the LORD say so, Whom He has redeemed from the hand of the enemy.
Psalm 107:2 NKJ

To live redeemed, you need to take control of the "hole beneath your nose." The power of confession is the agent that started the flow of God's grace that freed us from sin, transgression, and iniquity. As you continue to confess these truths, you will live redeemed and receive the full benefits of the new creation realities that have been given to you as your inheritance (2 Corinthians 5:17).

Confession is the most powerful tool in a Christian's arsenal. The tongue is the most powerful muscle in the human body; it is also the only muscle in the body that is connected on only one end. The solution, therefore, to controlling your tongue is to attach the loose end to the Holy Spirit and let Him have it.

Your tongue is the rudder of your ship, the yardstick of your success, and it will be the gavel during your judgment before

Perfect Redemption

Christ. James 3:6 says that it is a world of iniquity. Properly confessing the realities of the Word of God is the only way you can live above iniquity and the lies of the world.

Are you redeemed of the Lord? Has He redeemed you from the hand of the enemy? If your answers are yes, then say so. Say it now, say it often, and **say it loud!**

Let us begin making confessions that agree with the Word of God. As you continue to say them, you will believe them in your heart.

Say them now, say them often, and say them loud! And say them **out loud!**

I am redeemed by the Lord.

I have been redeemed from the hand of the enemy.

I have a new nature in Christ Jesus. The old man is dead.

I am new creature in Christ Jesus. Old things are passed away. Behold all things are new.

The scapegoat is dead: the old nature of sin and the old man is dead.

The living goat is alive: the new man is alive and I reckon myself to be alive.

I am redeemed, not by the blood of goats, but by the blood of Jesus.

Let the redeemed of the Lord say so.

I am redeemed of the Lord.

I say it now, I say it often, and I say it loud! And I say it **out loud!**

My covenant with my Father says that I am free from the power of darkness.

Let the Redeemed of the Lord Say So

Satan is under my feet because I am seated at the right hand of the Father of light.

I have authority over serpents and scorpions and over all the power of the enemy and nothing shall by any means hurt me.

I am redeemed from the hand of the enemy.

Let the redeemed of the Lord say so.

I am redeemed of the Lord.

I say it now, I say it often, and I say it loud! And I say it **out loud!**

The blood of Jesus has freed me from sin, transgression, and all iniquity.

The blood of Jesus is stronger than the blood of my fathers.

The blood of Jesus has been applied to the doorpost of my body, and sprinkled before the altar of incense of my soul and the mercy seat of my spirit.

Let the redeemed of the Lord say so.

I am redeemed of the Lord.

I say it now, I say it often, and I say it loud! And I say it **out loud!**

I have the covenant blessing of Abraham signed by the blood of Jesus.

I have the strength of the bull by the blood of Jesus.

Perfect Redemption

I have the tenacity of the goat by the blood of Jesus.

I have the obedience of the lamb by the blood of Jesus.

I have the innocence of the dove by the blood of Jesus.

I have authority over sickness and disease by the blood of Jesus.

I have authority over principalities and powers by the blood of Jesus.

By the blood of Jesus, my Father Yahweh is my Shepherd, Righteousness, Banner, Healer, Provider, and Protector.

Let the redeemed of the Lord say so.

I am redeemed of the Lord.

I say it now, I say it often, and I say it loud! And I say it **out loud!**

I have peace with God through faith in Jesus Christ.

I am complete in Him, who is the Head of all principalities and powers.

I am righteous through faith in Jesus Christ.

I have a lively hope of the resurrection from the dead as an eternal inheritance.

Let the redeemed of the Lord say so.

I am redeemed of the Lord.

I say it now, I say it often, and I say it loud! And I say it **out loud!**

Let the Redeemed of the Lord Say So

My tongue is the sword of the spirit.

My will is committed to God.

My soul is obedient to the Incarnate Word of God.

My body is the temple of the Holy Spirit.

My members are yielded instruments to the Holy Spirit.

I am a covenant-keeping disciple.

Let the redeemed of the Lord say so.

I am redeemed from the hand of the enemy.

I am redeemed of the Lord.

I live redeemed.

I am more than a conqueror through Him who loves me.

I am seated in the heavenlies.

I am a citizen of the kingdom of God.

I am not looking up. I am looking down.

Continue to confess these new creation realities in your life to live the freedom of the divine nature. The blood of Jesus has eternally sealed your spirit and you will live forever. You are redeemed of the Lord.

> *Let the redeemed of the LORD say so, Whom He has redeemed from the hand of the enemy.*
>
> *Psalm 107:2 NKJ*

PERFECT REDEMPTION

I am redeemed of the Lord.

I say it now, I say it often, and I say it loud. And I say it **out loud!**

I will continue to confess my victory by the blood of Jesus.

I have received perfect redemption!

Notes

1. *The Living Webster Encyclopedic Dictionary of the English Language*. Chicago, IL: The English Language Institute of America, 1977.

2. *The Living Webster Encyclopedic Dictionary of the English Language*. Chicago, IL: The English Language Institute of America, 1977.

3. E. W. Bullinger, "Appendix 10: The Spiritual Significance of Numbers," in *The Companion Bible* (London, England: Samuel Bagster and Sons Limited, 1972).

4. The blood of bulls and goats was used on the Day of Atonement to signify the forgiveness of sins, iniquities and transgressions for reconciliation to God. Lamb's blood was used on Passover for forgiveness of sins, iniquities and transgressions to signify covenant protection.

5. The word for "took part" in Hebrews 2:14 is the Greek word *metecho* which means to take only a part. "Partakers," in the earlier part of the verse is *koinoneo*, which means to fully share. In other words, children partake of flesh and blood, meaning both parts, but Jesus only took a part of mankind—the flesh—the blood came from God.

6. Angels being dispatched from the sanctuary is understood from compiling scriptures such as Psalm 20:1–2; Matthew 4:11; Mark 1:13; Revelation 3:5; Daniel 10:5–21, and Hebrews 1:13–14. Angels are ministering spirits sent to minister for those individuals that are about the Father's business.

7. William D. Edwards, MD; Wesley J. Gabel, Mdiv; and Floyd E. Hosmer, MS, AMI, "On the Physical Death of Jesus Christ," *Journal of American Medical Association* 255, no. 11 (March 21, 1986): 1455–1463.

This is an outstanding article by these medical professionals. A large portion of the clinical information contained in this chapter was taken from this source. Full acknowledgement, credit, and appreciation are due.

8. E. W. Bullinger, "Appendix 10: The Spiritual Significance of Numbers," in *The Companion Bible* (London, England: Samuel Bagster and Sons Limited, 1972).

9. Dale M. Sides, "Healing in the Passover," *Episkopos*, EP27, (Bedford, VA: Liberating Ministries for Christ International (L.M.C.I.), 2000).

10. "The Gospel of Nicodemus," in *The Lost Books of the Bible and the Forgotten Books of Eden* (World Bible Publishers, Inc., 1974).

11. William D. Edwards, MD; Wesley J. Gabel, Mdiv; and Floyd E. Hosmer, MS, AMI, "On the Physical Death of Jesus Christ," *Journal of American Medical Association* 255, no. 11 (March 21, 1986): 1456.

12. Dale M. Sides, "Redeemed From the Curse of Poverty," *Liberating Partners*, LP10 (Bedford, VA: L.M.C.I., 1998).

13. For more information on this subject, see *Mending Cracks in the Soul* by Dale M. Sides.

14. E. W. Bullinger, "Appendix 44: The Synonymous Words for 'Sin,' 'Transgression,' 'Iniquity,'" in *The Companion Bible* (London, England: Samuel Bagster and Sons Limited, 1972). This gives the Hebrews words for each of these concepts and a more thorough explanation about each of them.

15. Burton Stokes and Lynn Lucas, "Iniquity," in *No Longer a Victim* (Shippensburg, PA: Destiny Image Publishers, 1988). A further conversation with the author, Burton Stokes, has contributed to this conclusion.

16. The bastard curse is cited from Deuteronomy 23:2. The account of Judah and his daughter-in-law is found in Genesis 38.

17. 1 Kings 11:3–4, 11

18. Exodus 20:4–5; 13:8–11; 14

19. For more information on this subject, see *Covenant Healing in Communion* by Dale M. Sides.

Scripture Index

John

3:16, 8
8:32, 3, 9
8:36, 4
14:6, 24, 48, 136, 145
14:26, 153
16:7, 146
16:7–9, 51
16:8, 146, 153
17:17, 160
17:21–23, 14–15
19:28, 139
19:29, 41, 138
19:30, 139
19:34, 42, 68

Acts

13:8, 152
13:9, 152

Romans

1:29–32, 117
3:23, 30
3:25, 3, 10, 31
4:7, 95
5:1, 170
5:9, 140, 160, 170
5:12, 72
5:17, 31, 79
6:4, 127
6:6, 123, 124
6:11, 124

6:13, 56
8:2, 116
8:16, 146, 168
8:22–23, 67
8:24, 67
9:1, 146, 168
10:9–10, 133
10:17, 9
12:2, 164
14:10, 133
14:23b, 100

1 Corinthians

1:30, 11, 128, 157
5:7, 131, 138, 177
5:7–8, 160, 161
7:10–13, 60
11:23–25, 178
11:26, 178
11:27, 178
11:28–30, 179
15:33, 162

2 Corinthians

5:17, 127, 187
5:21, 72
7:1, 66
10:5, 163

Galatians

3:13, 48
3:14, 22, 23

Books and Booklets
by Dale M. Sides

*40 Days of Communion
in Your Home*

*Approved of God—by Grace
or by Works*

Devil, Give Me Back My Money!

Diverse Kinds of Tongues

*Flowing in All Nine Gifts
of the Holy Spirit*

God Damn Satan

Mending Cracks in the Soul

The Anointing In and On

The Ministry of Liberality

The Three Doctrines of Damnation

*True Confessions of Spiritual
Warriors*

*Understanding and Breaking
the Schemes of the Devil*

Utilizing Gift Ministries

*You Don't Have to Be Smart
to Walk with God*

The Lord gave the word: great was the company of those that published it.
Psalm 68:11

Liberating Publications, Inc.

PO Box 974 ❖ Bedford, VA 24523-0974 USA

(540) 586-2622 Phone ❖ (540) 586-9372 Fax

www.liberatingpublications.com

ORDER FORM

Qty.	Description	Price	Ext. Price
	Subtotal		
	Sales Tax*		
	S&H		
	Total Order		

*Virginia residents add 4.5% sales tax.

Standard Sh	
Orders under $25.00	Add $3.95
Orders $25.01 – $75.00	Add $5.95
Orders over $75.00	Add $7.95

(Please call for expedited delivery rates.)

Name _____

Address _____

City, State, ZIP _____

Daytime Phone _____

Payment ___Check ___VISA ___Master Card

Card # _____ Exp. _____

Signature _____

(You may wish to photocopy this page for future use.)